D0915909

DID DARWIN
GET IT RIGHT?

DID DARWIN GET IT RIGHT?

Catholics and the Theory of Evolution

George Sim Johnston

Our Sunday Visitor Publishing Division
Our Sunday Visitor, Inc.
Huntington, Indiana 46750

The author and publisher are grateful to all copyright holders without whose material this work could not have been completed, and whose credits can be found in the bibliography. Special thanks to *Crisis, Envoy,* and *Lay Witness,* publications in which portions of this work first appeared in a different form. If any copyrighted materials have been inadvertently used in this work without proper credit being given in one manner or another, please notify Our Sunday Visitor in writing so that future printings of this work may be corrected accordingly.

International Standard Book Number: 0-87973-945-2
Library of Congress Catalog Card Number: 98-65867

Cover design by Monica Watts

PRINTED IN THE UNITED STATES OF AMERICA

945

For Lisa

Contents

A Note to the Reader

This book was written in response to the widespread confusion among Catholics about how to deal with the theory of evolution. While the book may be read with profit by scholars, it is aimed at the general reader and supposes no technical knowledge about either science or theology. In making the book as "reader friendly" as possible, I have forgone the use of footnotes. In my experience, there are readers who shy away from books with footnotes, and I want this book to have as wide a circulation as possible. All of the quotes that I have used may be found in the books and articles listed in the bibliography. Readers who cannot find a particular citation may send an e-mail request for it at gsjohnston@compuserve.com.

Introduction

A few years ago, a Catholic friend of mine visited a dying relative in the hospital. The old woman had led a good life, but could not see her way to a belief in God. She was not a militant atheist, simply an agnostic, like so many modern people. God, in her view, had not given enough "proof" that he exists. My friend gently tried to argue the point, but to no avail. Finally, she produced the trump card that so often ends these discussions: "But, Jim, evolution has been proved by science. So the Bible can't be true!"

No issue is more difficult for Christian apologetics than evolution. Even highly educated Catholics can be at a loss to explain how the creation account in Genesis squares with what modern science tells us about the origin of man and other living beings.

Some Catholics take Darwin's account at face value and dismiss the early chapters of Genesis as myth or allegory. Others simply dig in their heels and refuse to accept any scientific datum, including the dating of fossils, that does not fit a literal reading of Genesis. For these "creationists" — Catholic as well as Protestant — it is evolution, and not the Book of Genesis, that is the fairy tale.

The hostility among Christians toward Darwin is understandable. His *Origin of Species*, first published in 1859, is a subversive book. It succeeded in undermining religious faith far more effectively than anything written by Marx or Freud. The idea that we are a chemical accident, the result of a blind, random process that did not have us in mind, is, as one fervent Darwinist puts it, "dangerous." It is an acid that eats through everything, dissolving religion and morality and leaving a Creator with nothing to do — at least in the realm of biology. If nature, as St. Paul teaches, is our stepladder to God, what Darwin and his disciples did was to pull down the ladder and chop it into pieces.

In dealing with a theory like Darwin's, Catholics should anchor themselves in a simple proposition: There can be no real conflict between faith and the legitimate findings of science. Truth is indivisible, and the works of God cannot contradict what he has chosen to reveal through Scripture and Tradition. The danger occurs when scientists trespass into theology or vice versa. The Galileo affair is a sobering reminder of what can happen when certain parties in the Church resist a scientific hypothesis on *a priori* biblical grounds. If the Congregation of Cardinals that condemned Galileo had paid more attention to Augustine and Aquinas, who both held that Scripture is not meant to teach a system of astronomy, the disastrous split that occurred between religion and science in the seventeenth century might have been avoided.

Today, science and religion are like two armed camps gazing suspiciously at one another across a huge metaphysical divide. But the fact is, they have much to talk about. Modern science, in the words of Chesterton, is speeding toward the mysteries of faith with the speed of an express train. Catholic theologians are quite comfortable in the finite, highly intricate, roughly twelve-billion-year-old universe described by modern cosmology.

Yet, the average person's understanding of these matters remains stuck in the nineteenth century. This is also true of many scientists. Francis Bacon accurately described the problem: A little science leads one away from God, while more science brings one back again. Most modern people have yet to make this U-turn. Their rejection of the supernatural is not even based on a dim memory of high-school physics and biology. Rather, it is on the level of those anti-clerical journalists a hundred years ago who asked how anyone in an age of steam engines and telegraphs can believe in a transcendent deity.

The great "scientific" stumbling block for Christian belief remains the disagreement between the creation account in Genesis 1 and the sciences of geology and paleontology. Darwin himself discarded a mild Protestant faith when he concluded that the author of Genesis was a bad geologist. To his mind, the biblical six days of creation and Lyell's *Principles of Geology* could not both be true. And this discomfort with the text of Genesis has not been restricted to the educated classes. According to the famous French worker-priest Abbé Michonneau, the apparent conflict between science and the six-day creation account promoted atheism among the poor far more effectively than any social injustice. Darwinian evolution is still the major ingredient of that "science."

Most educated people with a smattering of scientific knowledge regard every aspect of Darwin's theory as "proved." This is understandable, as both the media and the academy treat it as a self-evident truth on the order of Newton's law of gravity. Darwin's shrinkage of man to matter also makes him appealing to postmodern intellectuals, who in a pinch can dispense with Marx and Freud. Richard Rorty, our most fashionable academic philosopher, has, in a revealing phrase, declared his "faith" in Darwin. In the wake of the collapse of political Marxism, there has been a striking "flight to Darwin" among intellectuals. They now inundate us with books and articles championing Darwin's theory of natural selection as the key to all phenomena. Apparently, the cultural elite feel the need to prop up the last remaining pillar of nineteenth-century materialism.

But a large irony hangs over their enthusiasm. Darwin's theory is due for retirement within the next generation — not because of the attacks of creationists, but because scientists themselves now have serious reservations. The word "crisis" is not too strong to describe the current predicament among geneticists, paleontologists, and molecular biologists who call themselves evolutionists. While the idea of evolution will no doubt survive, the Darwinian explanation of that process, which is the only one we have, is finished. Leading evolutionists refuse to write its obituary for reasons that have more to do with their philosophical commitments than with hard science.

Although you wouldn't know it from reading the standard textbooks, Darwin has always had his detractors in the scientific community, especially outside the Anglo-Saxon countries. A majority of French biologists, for example, have never bought Darwin. But lately even in America and England the scientific debate over evolution has become, in the words of one participant, "sharp and frequently acrimonious." The conflict is for the most part hidden from the public. The refrain, formulated years ago by a prominent Darwinist, is that "the difficulties which weigh upon the professional biologist need not trouble the layman." Many of Darwin's disciples, moreover, are hesitant about taking their objections public for fear of being labeled "creationists."

But even in America, where a widespread aversion to Christian fundamentalism makes Darwin very appealing, biologists and paleontologists have begun to question his theory, albeit in books and journals that are not read by the general public. In this regard, the recent success of Dr. Michael Behe's *Darwin's Black Box* is significant; it is the first anti-Darwinist book written by a scientist to be published by a mainstream American publisher in decades. Other scientists who have a problem with Darwin prefer to remain quiet, however, since they don't wish to be quoted in a creationist tract. This silence leaves the field wide open to fervent materialists like the late Carl Sagan. Sagan could get away with telling the millions who watched the PBS series *Cosmos* that all species, including man, came into being by a process whose mechanism is perfectly transparent to modern science, because protests are seldom forthcoming from scientists who know better.

Despite the stranglehold on the media by popularizers like Sagan, it is quite possible that in the next generation Darwin will join Marx and Freud on the heap of discarded nineteenth-century ideologies. The empirical evidence against Darwin is so compelling that a paradigm shift is inevitable. His retirement will open the way for a return to traditional metaphysics. Philosophers can close the *Origin* and open their Aristotle or Aquinas — and do everyone a great service. Modern man will no longer be obliged to view himself as a shifting, accidental thing with no more dignity than a stone or jellyfish. Biology will be freed from the straitjacket of mechanistic philosophy and, more importantly, the doctrine of creation, whose eclipse in recent generations has had a devastating effect on Christian apologetics, will be restored to its rightful place. To borrow a phrase of Stanley Jaki's, Darwin took the metaphysical sting out of nature, and it is time to put it back.

This book is no diatribe against science. The Second Vatican Council rightly emphasized that science has its legitimate sphere of autonomy. Catholics ought to look forward to its discoveries with confidence and enjoyment. (The application of these discoveries, especially in the area of biotechnology, is another matter.) But I shall question the philosophical attitude that Jacques Maritain aptly dubbed "scientism." Scientism is the belief that there is no truth outside of what can be demonstrated by the natural sciences. Scientism asserts that the universe is self-explanatory, that all phenomena, including human consciousness, can be reduced to chemistry — or, ultimately, particle physics. This savage reductionism is a gross misreading of creation and of man in particular. Its chief intellectual prop is Darwin. When presented with facts that seem to contradict Darwin's scenario, the disciples of scientism often behave like devout religionists whose faith has been challenged. Some get belligerent; others become cagey. Still others have been known to blurt out, "There is no God, therefore it *had* to be that way." This, however, is not science, but "scientism" of a very crude sort.

It is this "scientistic" dogmatism, rather than science itself, which has created such a poisonous atmosphere for religious faith in our time. We live in a culture that accepts a truth only if it comes in scientific wrapping. Scientists themselves are often the chief victims of this mentality. They pay little heed to James Clerk Maxwell, the great Cambridge physicist, who warned: "One of the severest tests of a scientific mind is to discern the limits of the legitimate application of the scientific method." This is why it has been left to nonscientists, ranging from Christian apologists like G. K. Chesterton to agnostic philosophers like Karl Popper, to blow the whistle on the often extravagant claims made by modern evolutionists about what they actually know about the origin of living things.

Mention of Chesterton, a guide and mentor, brings up an important point. Can a nonscientist claim any credibility in questioning a scientific theory as entrenched as Darwinian evolution? The answer is — yes. One of the reassuring discoveries I made in examining the debate over evolution is that every aspect of the subject is accessible to the layman. All the major evolutionary writing, from Darwin and Huxley to Richard Dawkins and Stephen Jay Gould, has been aimed at the public. There is a reason for this. These writers are crusading materialists who wish to convert everyone to their view of things. They necessarily have to state their case in clear, nontechnical terms. There are no complicated mathematical models or paleontological arcana that have not been predigested for the educated layman. Evolution is, in one respect, the most literary of all the scientific theories.

So the debate over evolution invites trespassers from the humanist camp. And, in fact, there has been a line of enlightened amateurs — Samuel Butler, G. K. Chesterton, Hilaire Belloc, Arthur Koestler, Arnold Lunn, Norman Macbeth, Phillip Johnson — whose commonsense criticisms of Darwin often anticipate those of scientists. The layman who is willing to do some homework should feel no hesitation about plunging into this subject.

Since Darwin's apologists have few inhibitions about displaying a flippant agnosticism, I ought to put my own cards on the table and state that I am an orthodox Catholic. It is my contention that the public has been erroneously led to believe that in the debate over evolution the only choice available is between Bible-thumping fundamentalists and Darwin. As is often the case, there is a reasonable Catholic middle ground between the poles of biblical and scientific absolutism. It is a ground that was claimed by St. Augustine and is comfortably occupied by modern Catholic thinkers like Chesterton, Maritain, and Gilson. It is also where the Magisterium locates itself, especially during the pontificate of John Paul II, who has a keen interest in science.

To the argument that a believing Christian cannot approach the subject of evolution with objectivity, let me point out that the determination of Darwinists to rid the universe of a Creator makes their own claims of objectivity somewhat spurious. The tenacity of Darwin's theory among scientists and educators can only be explained by its crude materialism. Darwin's great German disciple August Weissmann declared that natural selection must be defended as the cause of evolution in no matter what fashion because "it is the only alternative to design." The biologist Julian Huxley claimed that Darwin's greatest achievement was to remove the idea of a Creator from intelligent discourse. His famous grandfather, T. H. Huxley, was more explicit; he wrote that the great merit of evolutionary theory is its "complete and irreconcilable antagonism to that vigorous and consistent enemy of the highest intellectual, moral, and social life of mankind — the Catholic Church."

I could supply pages of such quotations. The insistent atheism (and, in some cases, Marxism) of contemporary Darwinists like Haldane, Simpson, Gould, Lewontin, Dawkins, and E. O. Wilson is well known. These scientists start with a philosophical premise: There is no God. This allows them to rule out the possibility of design and purpose in nature. It imposes a teleological taboo, which in biology makes Darwin the winner by default. No matter how much evidence is adduced that the major evolutionary jumps — from reptile to mammal, for example — cannot have been the result of a gradual accumulation of genetic copying errors, they cling vehemently to the Darwinian scenario. This is why Karl Popper, hardly a creationist, called Darwinism a "metaphysical research program," a remark that cuts deeply with many Darwinists.

Philosophical materialists, if they wish to remain such, cannot be open-minded about the truth of Darwin's explanation of the origin of species. But a Catholic who is not a strict biblical literalist — who, in other words, reads the Bible with the mind of the Church — *can* be open-minded. If, moreover, he has been schooled in the philosophy of St. Thomas Aquinas, he can be serenely confident that philosophical rigor — not to mention plain common sense — can sort out the major issues that seem to separate religion and science. Common sense, Chesterton observed, has become an extinct branch of most scientific disciplines. A modest aim of this book is to suggest its reintroduction in the area of evolutionary biology.

There is one point in the debate over evolution that should be clarified from the start: The layman has to make a distinction between "evolution" and "Darwinism," something that is seldom done in the English-speaking world.

"Evolution" is the idea that all life-forms share common ancestors, and maybe even a single ancestor. This is a reasonable, if unproven, hypothesis. It is reasonable not because anyone has ever seen a species turn into a new one (one hasn't), but because all life-forms share certain genetic material and there are nested hierarchies of structure within the major animal groups. "Evolution" means common descent, but does not tell how it happened. It does not answer the question "How did an amoeba floating around the primordial soup eventually turn into *Homo sapiens?*"

"Darwinism" tries to answer that question by supplying a mechanism for evolution. This mechanism is natural selection working on random mutations.

The controversy in the seminar rooms and scientific journals is not over evolution *per se*, but over the means by which it happened. Either life-forms came about by blind chance or they did not. Darwin's theory of natural selection is the only one available that purports to explain how *Homo sapiens* and other species are the result of a blind, mechanical process. This is why the debate over Darwin's theory, and not evolution itself, is so important. It is Darwin's theory, moreover, and no other, that is taught in our schools. The fact that most writing on the subject makes no distinction between "evolution" and "Darwinism" only confuses the issue to the advantage of the materialist camp.

In addition to examining the merits of Darwin's case, this book will try to provide an intelligent Catholic's guide to the creation account in the first chapter of Genesis. No part of the Bible has proved such an obstacle to the modern mind. Educated Catholics are by no means exempt from the general muddle over how to read Genesis 1. The great papal encyclicals on biblical exegesis, starting with Leo XIII's *Providentissimus Deus* (1893), would be a great help, but it is safe to say that most Catholics have never heard of them. The Magisterium's teaching that there can be no real conflict between Scripture and science has never been properly absorbed by the laity — or by certain theologians, for that matter. Nor has its insistence that the Bible often uses figurative language and is not a textbook in geology or astrophysics. The result has been a kind of schizophrenia, which considers the first chapters of Genesis to be both the inerrant word of God and a scientific embarrassment.

Catholics in reality have no cause to be timid about Scripture or science. They simply need to distinguish between two different orders of knowledge — theological and scientific — and allow each its due competence. They should be extremely cautious about mixing the two. Putting God in the gaps unexplained by science has always been a mistake, because science often fills those gaps with material explanations. An enlightened Catholic view of science must recognize that God prefers to work through secondary causes. He concedes an enormous degree of causality to his creation, and we ought to be pleased as science explains more and more of it.

The Church's quarrel with many scientists who call themselves evolutionists is not about evolution itself, but rather about the philosophical materialism that is at the root of so much evolutionary thinking. John Paul II puts the matter succinctly: "The Church is not afraid of scientific criticism. She distrusts only preconceived opinions that claim to be based on science, but which in reality surreptitiously cause science to depart from its domain."

This remark was aimed at biblical exegetes, but it certainly applies to Darwinian science, which depends on hidden philosophical additives to reach its conclusions.

The stakes in the debate over Darwinian evolution are high. Darwinism refuses to recognize that there is, in John Paul II's words, an "ontological leap" between the rest of the animal kingdom and man. The clash between Christianity and modern evolutionary materialism finally involves two irreconcilable views of the human person. Humans are not brute animals; we are created in the image of God; and the place to look for a truly humanist ethic is not the rest of the animal kingdom, but in the other direction, at the three persons of the Holy Trinity in the act of eternal, mutual self-giving.

But we first have to clear away the intellectual debris that has accumulated in the century and a half since Darwin published his *Origin of Species*.

Chapter One

Solving the "Mystery of Mysteries": Darwin and His Theory

The Darwin Family

So many myths have been spun around the figure of Darwin and the history of his theory that untangling them can be difficult. History, as they say, is written by the victors, and most encyclopedias, textbooks, and popular histories simply repeat the prevailing Darwinian orthodoxy. Darwin himself has thus far been immune to the intense biographical scrutiny that has devastated the reputations of many leaders of the modernist revolt. While Marx and Freud, the two other members of the trinity governing the contemporary mind, are now widely regarded as ideologues who masqueraded as scientists, Darwin still has the reputation of being an honest man of science whose close observations of nature led him to embrace with reluctance his bombshell theory.

Darwin's private notebooks, which were not fully published until the 1970s, tell a different story. Darwin was a philosophical materialist long before the publication of the *Origin*. By the late 1830s, when he was developing his theory of natural selection, he had already, in the words of two recent biographers, Desmond and Moore, "embraced a terrifying materialism." His covert notebooks from this period are full of jottings about how the human mind, morality, and even belief in God are mere artifacts of the brain's chemistry: ". . . love of the deity [is the] effect of organization, oh you Materialist!" he wrote to himself at one point. Darwin had no problem dispensing with a light Protestant faith early in life, and he became increasingly hostile toward religion as he grew older. One historian has described him as a "good Christian," but this hardly fits the man who wrote in his journal in 1873: "I have lately read Morley's *Life of Voltaire* and he insists strongly that direct attacks on Christianity (even when written with the wonderful force and vigor of Voltaire) produce little permanent effect: real good seems only to follow the slow and silent side attacks."

In looking for an explanation of Darwin's distaste for Christianity, one might plausibly start with his family. By the time he was born, a strong antipathy toward revealed religion had been running in the male Darwin line for two generations. The Darwins were part of England's rising class of wealthy Whigs, the manufacturers and merchants who were pushing aside the Tory establishment and its Anglican religion. Charles's paternal grandfather, Erasmus, was a freethinker and agnostic who wrote endless tracts and poems urging humanity to dispense with religion and find nourishment instead in "the milk of science." Erasmus could not abide even the lax Unitarianism of Charles's other grandfather, the pottery magnate Josiah Wedgwood, whose easygoing creed he acidly described as "a featherbed to catch a falling Christian."

Robert Darwin, son of Erasmus and father to Charles, was a highly successful doctor; he was also an atheist and a Freemason. He counseled his son Charles on the eve of the latter's wedding to hide from his wife whatever religious doubts he might have. Charles later wrote that he never doubted that what his cold, domineering father thought or did was "absolutely true, right and wise." Historian Gertrude Himmelfarb writes that the father's atheism made Charles's disbelief, when it came, a natural and acceptable mode of thought; more than that, "it seemed to enjoin disbelief precisely as a filial duty."

A School for Agnostics

Charles's education also encouraged a stark philosophical materialism. In 1826, while pursuing a desultory course of studies in Edinburgh, the seventeen-year-old Darwin became involved with a radical, freethinking group of students and professors. He attended debates and lectures in which supernatural faith was lampooned and all phenomena, including the human mind, were explained as solely the result of natural causes. "The illicit excitement of these meetings was enormous," Darwin's biographers write. "Established Church doctrines were being impugned, dissident sciences championed. It must have affected the impressionable seventeen-year-old. He was quick to take an active part."

Among Darwin's mentors at Edinburgh was a sharp-tongued, caustic naturalist named Robert Grant. Grant was the chief intellectual influence of Charles's late adolescence. "Nothing was sacred for Grant," Desmond and Moore write. "As a freethinker, he saw no spiritual power behind nature's throne. The origin and evolution of life were due simply to physical and chemical forces, all obeying natural laws."

As often happens, the young Darwin's mind managed to run along two tracks for some time. He still maintained the mild Protestantism of his mother's family while indulging in ever more venturesome speculations about the material basis of reality. He finally abandoned his faith altogether when he came to the conclusion that the emerging science of geology contradicted the creation account in Genesis. In later years, he was disgusted by the spectacle of liberal Anglican clergymen rushing to embrace his infidel ideas.

Scientific Agendas

Now, it may be argued that Darwin's hostility toward Christianity is beside the point. Shouldn't a scientific theory be judged on its own merits, rather than on the motives and psychology of its progenitor? Yes, of course — if the theory is truly scientific and confirmed by empirical observation. Isaac Newton was as strange as they come; as John Maynard Keynes pointed out, Newton's private philosophical notebooks make one think of an ancient Babylonian magician. But Newton's scientific theories were rigorously formulated. They can be tested and shown to be true for most of material reality. But an ideology dressed up as science is a different matter. Theories like Darwinism, Marxism, and Freudianism have an explanation for everything (natural selection, economic repression, the unconscious) and so finally explain very little; they are elastic and vague enough to absorb almost any contradiction; when they run into falsifying data, they simply mutate. And since these theories began, consciously or not, as highly skewed readings of the available evidence, the biographies of their founders are very much to the point.

It is the job of a scientist to explain things without reference to a Creator. Great scientists like Gregor Mendel, who deciphered the genetic basis of heredity, operate this way, and when evaluating Mendel's work, we don't need to know what he thought about God. His rigorous mathematical analysis of his breeding experiments with peas can be tested and verified on its own terms. Mendel happened to be an Augustinian monk, but it makes no difference. A Christian physicist or biologist who runs into an intractable problem is not obliged to throw up his arms and say, "Well, God did it that way." Rather, he waits patiently for a natural explanation. If such is not forthcoming, he admits a scientific mystery and humbly hands over his data to philosophers and theologians, who may then talk about design and creation.

At the same time, a scientist who takes the (often covert) position that because there is no God, any puzzling phenomenon can in principle be explained entirely by material causes is also out of bounds. As is the case with a Christian physicist who solves any mystery in nature by simply positing divine intervention, scientists who adopt this strategy are practicing bad philosophy rather than sound science. Many Darwinists take the position that because other material explanations (for example, Lamarckism: the inheritance of acquired characteristics) of evolution are false, Darwin's must be true. But they can only do this if they rule out of court nonmaterial first causes. As scientists, they are not qualified to do this. Science, which deals only with physical reality, can have nothing to say about what, if anything, is outside that reality.

The *Origin of Species* fits this category of a science book that is always letting philosophical materialism slip in unnoticed. Darwin's argument contains so many questionable assumptions, starting with his views about God, that it cannot be evaluated strictly as a work of hard science. It is not rigorously empirical in the way Mendel's "Experiments in Plant Hybridization" is. To pick up Mendel's concise and carefully reasoned paper after reading the circular and often cloudy arguments of the *Origin* is to enter a different realm of thought. Unlike Mendel's, Darwin's case depends on extrascientific suppositions, the first of which is that the explanation of all natural phenomena is strictly material.

Twenty years before the publication of the *Origin*, Darwin was a convinced materialist who wished to rid nature of a Creator. In other words, his agenda was not strictly scientific; it was metaphysical — or, we might say, counter-meta-physical. Darwin's materialism was antecedent to, and not a result of, his scientific work. Even so, his philosophical biases would not be an issue if his theorizing had, like Mendel's or Pasteur's, been limited to secondary and proximate causes. But Darwin was stalking the First Cause. It was, he confessed in a letter, like committing "murder." And this agenda must be taken into account when judging the argument of the *Origin*, because virtually every chapter of that book contains hidden and unwarranted philosophical assumptions.

Evolution Before Darwin

Contrary to popular belief, Darwin did not invent the idea of evolution. The idea that species might change into new ones over the course of time had been around since the ancient Greeks. In the early fifth century, St. Augustine proposed a kind of theory of evolution. In his great commentary, *De Genesi ad Litteram* (or *On the Literal Meaning of Genesis*), he speculated that in the beginning God had planted "rational seeds" (*rationes seminales*) in nature that eventually fructified into plants and animals. This would be "evolution" in the strict sense of the word, an unfolding of what is already there, like an acorn turning into an oak. Being directed and purposeful, however, St. Augustine's version of evolution is utterly non-Darwinian; it is, rather, creation on the installment plan.

A century before Darwin published his *Origin of Species* (1859), the French zoologist Buffon proposed evolution as a serious scientific theory. Buffon wrote that "with sufficient time" all living forms could have evolved from "one primordial type." A number of thinkers in France and England, including Darwin's paternal grandfather, Erasmus, began to champion the idea. Erasmus Darwin published a long scientific poem called *Zoonomia* (1797), in which he presented a rough outline of evolution that dispensed entirely with a Creator:

> First forms minute, unseen by spheric glass,
> Move on the mud, or pierce the watery mass;
> These, as successive generations bloom,
> New powers acquire, and larger limbs assume;
> Whence countless groups of vegetation spring,
> And breathing realms of fin, and feet, and wing.

In his autobiography, Darwin recounts how at Edinburgh in 1826 he was introduced to the idea of evolution by Doctor Grant: "I listened in silent astonishment, and as far as I can judge, without any effect on my mind. I had previously read 'Zoonomia' of my grandfather, in which similar views are maintained. . . ." Half-baked theories about evolution were part of the progressive intellectual baggage in England well before Darwin published his book. In 1844, a versatile journalist named Robert Chambers published a pseudo-scientific work, *Vestiges of the Natural History of Creation*, which argued that all organic life evolved from simple, primitive forms. The book was a best-seller and the subject of fashionable talk. In Benjamin Disraeli's novel *Tancred* (1847), the hero protests to a woman who urges the book on him, "I don't believe I ever was a fish." To which the lady replies: "Oh! But it's all proved. . . . First there was nothing; then there was something; then — I forget the next — I think there were shells; then fishes; then we came — let me see — did we come next?"

Theories of evolution were so commonplace in the middle of the nineteenth century that Darwin was afraid that his own version would be scooped by somebody else, as it very nearly was by Alfred Russell Wallace. The problem with these pre-Darwinian theories of evolution was that they asserted the fact of evolution without explaining how it had happened. (An exception would be Lamarck's problematic theory of acquired characteristics.) What put Darwin on the map was his explanation of *how* evolution had occurred. His epochal contribution was to come up with a mechanism whose simplicity and seemingly taut logic gave it immense appeal. This was the idea of "natural selection," to which he later appended Herbert Spencer's phrase, "survival of the fittest." It was so simple that the great Victorian biologist Thomas Huxley exclaimed, "How stupid not to have thought of that!"

Darwin's theory goes like this: Organisms produce offspring that vary slightly from their parents, and natural selection favors the survival of those individuals whose peculiarities (sharper teeth, more prehensile claws) render them best adapted to their environment. Although refinements have been added, this remains the core of Darwinian evolution: random variation as to raw material, and natural selection as the directing force. Add millions of years, and you get the incredible diversity of plants and animals we see today.

The usual PBS documentary has the lightbulb going off over Darwin's head while observing the animals on the Galápagos Islands in 1835 during the voyage of the *Beagle*. But the varieties of finches and other species he saw there merely gave him examples of small ecological changes within a species that he later used to buttress his argument. It was only in March 1837 that Darwin became an evolutionist, largely as a result of conversations with the ornithologist John Gould, and it was not until September 1838 that, after reading Thomas Malthus's *Essay on Population* (1798), he had his idea of natural selection.

Darwin's idea of natural selection came not so much

from his observations of nature, as from his reading of the great eighteenth-century British economists. It is, in this respect, a somewhat bookish theory. Adam Smith's "invisible hand," which directs the course of a capitalist economy without any forethought on the part of the economy's participants, operates very much like natural selection. But the *Eureka!* moment came when Darwin read Malthus's famous (and discredited) essay. "Here at last I had got a theory by which to work," he wrote later.

Malthus held that population tends to multiply faster than the food supply, and so there will always be a "struggle for existence" — a key phrase that Darwin appropriated — in which the weakest succumb to famine, disease, and war. Malthus's chief appeal to Darwin was his insistence that society is governed by the same sort of mechanical laws that Newton had demonstrated in physics. Malthusian man is hardly distinguishable from a billiard ball; he is an inert object, pushed about by external forces like disease and limited food supply. Darwin had the same deterministic agenda in biology — to describe the origin of species as the result of blind, mechanical laws rather than the willful act of a Creator. It is not surprising that Alfred Russell Wallace, the codiscoverer of evolution by natural selection, also came to the idea by way of Malthus.

The irony is that Malthus's *Essay* explicitly condemned the idea of evolution. Darwin, in fact, chose to support his theory of evolution with the same evidence that Malthus used against it — the experience of animal and plant breeders. Malthus noted how a breeder could only go so far with an animal before it reverted back to type, whereas Darwin insisted that the small changes observed in breeding pens could keep accumulating until new species appeared. This was the very core of his theory: the extrapolation of major evolutionary novelties from the small biological shifts that occur in species all the time.

The Art of Pigeon Breeding

Once he struck on his theory, Darwin spent a great deal of time observing animal breeders and fanciers at work in the "feather clubs" around London. The first fifty pages of the *Origin* are mainly about pigeons, which often surprises readers. Darwin noticed that through selective breeding, pigeons could be made to develop certain desired characteristics: color, wingspan, and so forth. Darwin extrapolated from these observations the notion that over huge expanses of time species could evolve by a similar process of selection, the only difference being that the "breeder" is nature itself, sifting out the weak, allowing the strong to multiply. Modern Darwinists like John Maynard Smith and Richard Dawkins still claim that this process is pretty much all that is needed to explain everything from the defense mechanism of the bombardier beetle to human consciousness.

But a crucial point has to be made here, one that is often raised by Darwin's scientific critics. What Darwin saw in the breeding pens is *microevolution.* Microevolution denotes the changes that occur within a species over time. Such evolution is not controversial. The mutations of bacteria in response to antibiotics are a well-known example. So are the varieties of finches that Darwin saw on the Galápagos. With no direct evidence — actually, with much evidence to the contrary — Darwin claimed that over long periods these "micro" changes could gradually add up to *macroevolution,* which are the really big jumps — from reptile to mammal to *Homo sapiens,* for example.

This is where his theory begins to run into problems. First, let's take a look at the fossil record.

Chapter Two

Darwin on the Rocks: What the Fossils Show

The Disturbing Gaps

There are two obvious places to look for verification of Darwin's theory that all plants and animals evolved gradually from some primordial life-form by means of natural selection: the fossil record and breeding experiments. If Darwin's theory is correct, the fossil record should show innumerable slight gradations between earlier species and later ones. In Darwin's own words, "the number of intermediate and transitional links, between all living and extinct species must have been inconceivably great."

But Darwin was aware that the fossil record of his day showed nothing of the sort. There were enormous discontinuities between all the major animal groups. This was not a matter of filling in the slots between starfish A and starfish B; the gaps between all major categories of animals and plants were huge and apparently systematic.

Darwin accordingly entitled his chapter on the subject, "On the Imperfection of the Fossil Record." He hoped that future digging would fill in the gaps, which he admitted to be the "most obvious and gravest objection which can be urged against my theory." The publication of the *Origin* sent whole armies of paleontologists into the folds of the earth to find the "innumerable" transitional links that Darwin said must be there. What did this army find? The answer appears to be — nothing. The fossil evidence does not support the idea that species evolved by minute gradations. Stephen Jay Gould, the Harvard paleontologist, calls this the great "trade secret" of modern paleontology.

The fossil record shows exactly what it showed in Darwin's day — that species appear suddenly in a fully developed state and change little or not at all before disappearing (ninety-nine out of one hundred species are extinct). Niles Eldredge, head of paleontology at the American Museum of Natural History, writes that the theory of gradual evolution "is out of phase" with the fossil record. Admits Gould, "Phyletic gradualism (i.e., gradual evolution) . . . was never seen in the rocks."

Biology's Big Bang

The earth is roughly 4.5 billion years old. Bacteria appeared 3.5 billion years ago. The nucleated cell arrived perhaps 1.2 billion years ago; its sudden advent, in the words of one scientist, "marks the greatest known discontinuity in the sequence of living things." These cells assembled somewhat haphazardly into algae and a few other oddities that seem to have played no part in later animal evolution. Then, about 550 million years ago, came biology's Big Bang. It occurred at the beginning of the Cambrian era. There was an explosion of highly organized life-forms — mollusks, jellyfish, trilobites — for which not a single ancestral fossil can be found in the earlier rocks. Richard Dawkins writes in *The Blind Watchmaker* that it "is as though they were just planted there, without any evolutionary history." The Precambrian strata, moreover, are perfectly suited for the imprinting of fossils. In some locations, there are over five thousand feet of unbroken layers of sedimentary rock; but they do not contain the innumerable transitional species that Darwin maintained to be there. They are, in fact, an evolutionary blank.

With the Cambrian, however, in a geological flash, there appeared more than one thousand genera, containing some five thousand species. All the major animal phyla —which are the basic body plans: vertebrates, invertebrates, and so forth — were suddenly swarming the seas. The famous Burgess Shale in the Canadian Rockies shows a riot of complex life-forms, much of it quite bizarre to modern eyes. And, contrary to Darwin's idea of progressive diversity, there has not been a single new phylum since. The post-Cambrian record shows a few species in many groups (or phyla) have been replaced over millennia by numerous species in a few groups. This is the reverse of Darwin's model. Adam Sedgwick, a famous British zoologist, said that the pattern of life on this planet actually seemed to be one of "devolution": All the archetypal forms appeared in an initial burst and seemed to "precipitate" later species as variations on a few themes.

Darwin wrote of the Cambrian explosion: "The case at present must remain inexplicable; and may be truly urged as a valid argument against [my theory]." The rapid appearance of multicellular organisms on the earth has become even more of a puzzle in recent decades. The duration of the Cambrian explosion was once thought to have been about forty million years, and scientists had difficulty explaining how all those jellyfish and trilobites could have formed from scratch in such a relatively brief span. Textbook phrases like "quantum evolution" or "adaptive radiation" did not explain the phenomenon — they merely described it. In 1993, the findings of a team of American and Russian geologists working in Siberia made the problem even thornier. They took careful radiometric readings of sediments containing the earliest Cambrian fossils. Their conclusion was that the entire Cambrian explosion occurred within five million to ten million years (and perhaps nearer the lower limit). As Gould puts it, "fast is much, much faster than we ever thought."

Five million years is a breathtakingly short span for a haphazard mechanism like natural selection to bring forth a range of animal types that far exceeds what we see today. The problem is even more striking when we consider the traditional Darwinist argument that, yes, the self-organization of complex life-forms does seem improbable, but, given vast stretches of time, natural selection can accomplish virtually anything. The time frame now available for evolution to have done all its basic body work is a geological blink of the eye. More importantly, there are no transitional forms, no gradations to speak of, leading up to these complex animals, any one of which, according to Darwin, would require innumerable evolutionary ancestors.

This compacting of the Cambrian explosion is a major problem for orthodox Darwinists. As Darwin wrote in the *Origin*, "If numerous species belonging to the same genera or families have really started into life all at once, the fact would be fatal to my theory of descent with slow modification through natural selection." Five million years is not, of course, "all at once" in common parlance, but it is close to being that in geological terms, especially if we are considering the diversification of some still unknown primitive cell into all the major categories of animal life.

The story is the same for plants, for which we have abundant fossils. Many land plants appeared about 450 million years ago with no apparent ancestry. Flowering plants, known as angiosperms, appeared about 120 million years ago. Their abrupt introduction puzzled Darwin, as it puzzles scientists today. Darwin wrote to his friend the botanist Joseph Hooker, "Nothing is more extraordinary in the history of the Vegetable Kingdom, as it seems to me, than the *apparently* very sudden or abrupt development of the higher plants." The fossil record of plants is every bit as discontinuous — and inexplicable in Darwinian terms — as that of animals.

Abrupt Appearances

What do animal fossils subsequent to the Cambrian period show? A man from Mars looking at the record of the last 540 million years would say that species are replaced by other species, rather than evolve into them. Steven Stanley, a paleontologist who teaches at Johns Hopkins, writes in *The New Evolutionary Time Table* that "the fossil record does not convincingly document a single transition from one species to another." And the higher we go in the taxonomic order, the greater the gaps in the record. All thirty-two orders of animals, for example, appear out of nowhere. This point could not be more important: The fossils do not show gradual evolution. Any number of well-known paleontologists and geologists may be quoted on the subject:

> Unfortunately, the origins of most higher categories are shrouded in mystery; commonly new higher categories appear abruptly in the fossil record without evidence of transitional ancestral forms. *(Raup and Stanley)*
>
> When a new phylum, class or order appears, there follows a quick, explosive (in terms of geological time) diversification so that practically all orders or families known appear suddenly and without any apparent transitions. *(Simpson)*
>
> Honesty compels us to admit that our ignorance concerning [the relationship of the higher animal taxa] is still great, not to say overwhelming. This is a depressing state of affairs considering that more than one hun-

dred years have passed since the great post-*Origin* period of phylogeny construction. *(Mayr)*

The evolutionary trees that adorn our textbooks
have data only at the tips and nodes of their branches;
the rest is inference, however reasonable, not the evidence of fossils. *(Gould)*

What about those pictures in museums and textbooks,
those charts showing how primitive life-forms gradually
evolved into higher species? Paleontologists, in effect, find a
fossil of an extinct species and make up a story connecting it
with a later or earlier animal. But they never find the transitional forms that Darwin's theory demands. The famous series of pictures from the American Natural History Museum
showing the "evolution" of horses, the diminutive *Eohippus*
(or *Hyracotherium*, "dawn horse") slowly changing into modern *Equus*, is now something of a historical curiosity. In 1905,
an exhibit was set up in the museum that showed the available horse fossils arranged according to size. These fossils
were taken from different times and places and put together
simply to demonstrate what evolution *might* have looked like.
The line of descent implied for these specimens is apocry-
phal. *Eohippus* remained *Eohippus*; it was followed by numerous species of horses, some larger, some smaller. Simpson
of Harvard calls the most famous of equid trends, the gradual
reduction of the side toes, "flatly fictitious. There was no such
trend. . . . " The horse chart is nonetheless widely reprinted
and passed off as fact. It remains the standard iconography
for Darwinian evolution.

The failure of the fossils to confirm Darwin has been a
sore point among paleontologists. Many choose to put a spin
on the fossil record to give the impression that it shows Darwinian gradualism. Niles Eldredge writes that for decades

this amounted to something like fibbing: "We paleontologists have said that the history of life supports that interpretation, all the while knowing that it does not."

Bushes and Ladders

In recent years paleontologists have retreated from simple connect-the-dot scenarios linking earlier and later species. Instead of ladders, they now talk of bushes. What we see in the fossils, according to this view, are only the twigs, the end products of evolution, while the key transitional forms that would give a clue about the origin of major animal and plant groups remain hidden. The gaps on the evolutionary trees occur at just the points where the crucial changes had to take place. The direct ancestors of all the major groups — reptiles, mammals, flowering plants — are missing. There is no fossil grandparent of the monkeys, for example. "Modern gorillas, orangutans, and chimpanzees spring out of nowhere," writes paleontologist Donald Johanson, discoverer of "Lucy." "They are here today; they have no yesterday." The same is true of bats, elephants, and turtles: They all simply burst upon the scene — *de novo*, as it were.

Once a species appears, moreover, it stubbornly remains what it is. Bacteria have been around for billions of years; some can replicate every fifteen minutes; and yet, bacteria are still bacteria. Like other species, they possess a certain elasticity that allows them to cope with changes in their environment. But nobody has ever seen them turn into something that is *not* a bacterium. Bees preserved in amber from millions of years ago are almost identical to modern bees. Horseshoe crabs, sharks, and lungfish have stuck to their original blueprint over even longer expanses of time despite significant shifts in their environments. All species, in fact, refuse to change much until their final exit, which is usually brought about by a mass or local extinction. Their departure, in other words, has more to do with bad luck than with losing a Darwinian struggle for survival.

In Germany, Otto Schindewolf, the most prominent paleontologist at mid-century, rejected Darwinism and stated flatly that the presumed intermediate forms do not exist. The gaps, according to Schindewolf, were in Darwin's theory, not in the fossils. This is not what the Darwinist camp wanted to hear, and so for decades the geneticists who control what John Maynard Smith calls the High Table of evolutionary discourse did not invite the fossil people to dinner. As Maynard Smith puts it, "Any paleontologist rash enough to offer a contribution to evolutionary theory [was told] to go away and find another fossil, and not to bother the grownups." Recently, combative paleontologists like Gould and Eldredge have brought their own chairs to the table, and there has been a food fight ever since.

The Eclipse of Paleontology

But for over a hundred years after the publication of the *Origin of Species* the discipline of paleontology was in eclipse because the data it provided did not support Darwin. As one historian of science has written, "The majority of paleontologists felt that their evidence simply contradicted Darwin's stress on minute, slow, and cumulative changes leading to species transformation." Hence, Oswald Spengler was able to write in *The Decline of the West* (1918-1922), "There is no more conclusive refutation of Darwinism than that furnished by paleontology." Both Stanley and Eldredge have written about how, beginning with T. H. Huxley, paleontologists have glossed over the fossil problem. Until the 1970s, the studies of young paleontologists eager to make a name for themselves showed nothing but abrupt appearance followed by stasis and as a result often went unpublished.

This is an example of what biologist W. R. Thompson meant when he wrote that "the success of Darwinism was accompanied by a decline in scientific integrity." Other examples would be the Piltdown Man fraud, which was perpetrated at the highest levels of England's scientific establishment, and Haeckel's fake drawings of embryological development. But the treatment of the fossil record is the most telling instance of philosophical corruption. A truly rigorous science would not adduce as evidence in support of a theory data that in reality contradicts it; nor would it talk with such assurance about the existence of transitional forms that are never found. As Chesterton quipped, Darwinists seem to know everything about missing links except for the fact that they are missing.

The continued invocation of "gaps" in the record, moreover, does not square with the opinion of many experts that the fossil record is sufficient as it stands. Eldredge and Tattersall write, "One hundred and twenty years of paleontological research later, it has become abundantly clear that the fossil record will not confirm this part [the existence of close transitional forms] of Darwin's predictions. Nor is the problem a miserably poor record. The fossil record simply shows that this prediction was wrong." Michael Denton, a molecular biologist, writes that the fossil record "is not as bad as is often maintained," pointing out, for example, that a very high percentage of fossils for living terrestrial vertebrates has been found. David Raup, a statistical paleontologist at the University of Chicago, writes that we now have "a quarter of a million fossil species, but the situation hasn't changed. . . . "

Darwin himself admitted that such conclusions would

by themselves invalidate his theory of gradual evolution via natural selection. "He who rejects [my] view of the imperfection of the geological record, will rightly reject the whole theory." As we shall see, a number of paleontologists in the 1970s came up with an *ad hoc* explanation of the gaps in the record in order to save the theory. It may be argued, however, that the true purpose of "punctuated equilibrium," as that explanation is called, is to shelter the theory from empirical falsification by insisting that all major evolutionary events take place off stage where they cannot be observed. In this, paleontologists like Gould and Eldredge were simply following the strategy of Darwin himself in later editions of the *Origin*, where he argued that since the crucial events of evolution are hidden, his theory cannot be refuted. One of Darwin's early scientific critics complained that this was the first time in the history of science that ignorance was adduced as an argument. But as the subsequent history of Darwinism shows, it was not to be the last.

Chapter Three

The Sex Life of Fruit Flies: Other Problems with Darwin's Theory

What the Breeders Show

Since we don't see species gradually changing into other species in the fossil record, the other obvious place to look is breeding experiments. Darwin himself had a keen interest in the experience of breeders. He spent long hours talking to them and taking notes. The changes and improvements that breeders could bring about in a species were an important datum for the formulation of his theory and a centerpiece of his argument in the *Origin of Species.*

But there was a problem. The changes he witnessed in the breeding pens were trivial compared to the transformations demanded by a theory meant to explain the *origin* of species. Slight, or even dramatic, modifications of existing organs do not add up to macroevolution. In fact, the evidence of breeders really went against Darwin. Breeders can change the color of a pigeon or the size of a pig to some degree, but they can only go so far. In fact, all breeders have the same experience: If they try to go too far in one direction, the animal or plant in question either becomes sterile or reverts back to type. Dogs remain dogs, fruit flies remain fruit flies.

The most famous breeder of all, Luther Burbank, found no evidence of the unlimited plasticity of species that Darwin's theory demands and posited a Law of Reversion to Average: "I know from my experience that I can develop a plum half an inch long or one 2 ½ inches long, with every possible length in between, but I am willing to admit that it is hopeless to try to get a plum the size of a small pea, or one as big as a grapefruit. . . . Experiments . . . have given us scientific proof of what we had already guessed by observation; namely, that plants and animals all tend to revert in successive generations, toward a given mean or average. . . . In short, *there is undoubtedly a pull toward the mean which keeps all living things within some more or less fixed limitations.*" (Italics mine.)

Even if breeders were able to produce a genuinely new organ or species, it would still not prove Darwin's case, because the guidance of intelligent agents such as breeders is hardly an example of a random, mindless process. What is relevant, however, is the fact that when animals who have been bred for special characteristics are released to their natural habitat, their descendants lose those characteristics and revert to the original stock. Animal breeders, then, can be cited only as witnesses against Darwin. When Darwin wrote his book, there was already a voluminous literature testifying that species are hard-edged, that they have limits beyond which they do not go. Darwin knew this literature well. How did he deal with it in the *Origin*?

Darwin dispensed with the experience of breeders in one short paragraph. He stated that it is "rash to assert that a limit had been attained in any case." This was often his way of dealing with contradictory evidence: Deny its validity — or simply mention it and then put it aside. His modern scientific disciples often use the same strategy. Anyone familiar with their writings knows the value they ascribe to what they call the "predictive" power of the theory. If breeders were ever to show one species changing into another, or even developing a single new organ, such an occurrence would be the centerpiece of Darwinian literature. High-school biology texts would present it as confirming a "prediction" made by the theory. But since breeding experiments only demonstrate the fixed boundaries of species, the subject is quietly dropped.

Genetic Packages Within Limits

Darwin was quite correct in pointing out the dramatic variability of certain species. All dogs, for example, are probably descended from a single mongrellike stock that lived thousands of years ago. The animals themselves seem aware of this; a puppy of any breed at once recognizes a dog of any other breed as his own kind. Moreover, all varieties of dog are interfertile, although disparity of size can prevent mating. But this "variation" within a species is not "evolution." "Evolution" means the appearance of genuine novelties. "Variation" is simply change within the strict limits of an already existing type. Dog breeders have been at work since ancient Egypt, and not one has ever produced an animal that does not present every feature that characterizes a dog.

Geneticists, who have spent decades zapping fruit flies with X rays in order to rearrange their chromosomes, report the same phenomenon: No matter how many disturbances they create in the relatively simple chromosomes of a fruit fly, producing effects that range from an increase in bristles to freaks with legs protruding from the head, they still have never seen a fruit fly turn into anything other than a fruit fly. Regarding the endless fruit-fly experiments, Pierre P. Grasse, the famous French zoologist, writes: "The fruit fly (*drosophila melanogaster*, the favorite pet insect of geneticists) . . . seems not to have changed since the remotest times." The unavoidable conclusion is that DNA programs a species to remain stubbornly what it is. And this is confirmed by the fossils: Once a species appears, there are minor fluctuations around a norm, often for millions of years, and nothing more.

The late Richard Goldschmidt, a leading geneticist who taught at Berkeley, spent years observing the mutations of fruit flies and concluded that biologists had to give up Darwin's idea that an accumulation of micro-changes creates new species. If you have a "thousand-point" mutation in a fruit fly, a statistical impossibility, it is still a fruit fly. Goldschmidt was the target of a savage campaign of vilification for pointing this out, but Stephen Jay Gould now claims that he was on the right track after all in asserting that scientists were getting nowhere with micro-changes adding up to major evolutionary jumps.

The relatively small changes we do see in species, such as wolves growing a heavier coat in a colder climate, or the beak of the finch adapting to the size of available seeds, tend to *preserve* a species rather than transform it into something brand-new. These small ecological adjustments don't seem to go very far, except in the minds of Darwinists, who view them as exhibiting the entire process that created wolves and birds in the first place.

Reptiles into Birds

Take the finch, one of the canonical subjects of evolutionary literature. A few years ago, a science writer named Jonathan Weiner wrote a book about his time on the Galápagos Islands with two scientists, a couple named Grant, who study these birds. The Grants spent years measuring and recording the varieties of finches on the islands in order to observe "evolution in action." A population shift took place in the aftermath of a drought; it resulted in relatively more large-beaked finches, who had an easier time opening the tougher seeds that survived the lack of water. Then the floods came, finches died off, and in the next generation the balance shifted in favor of finches with smaller beaks, who could peck at the tiny seeds that were available again. So we leave the finches pretty much as we found them. But the lesson for Weiner is that "evolution" is going on all around us. If he had used "ecological adjustment" for "evolution" the book would be less misleading — but then the Pulitzer jury, which gave *The Beak of the Finch* its science prize, would presumably have been less impressed.

Weiner's book would be more helpful if it explained how reptiles turned into birds in the first place. Even a partial list of what this would have involved makes it clear why Darwinists use fuzzy word pictures when discussing the really big leaps between animal groups. The late Norman Macbeth, a brilliant skeptic with no creationist axe to grind, pointed out several of the apparently insuperable difficulties involved in a step-by-step transformation of a reptile into a bird. To grasp how much the scenario entails, Macbeth writes, we have to consider at least the following: "The development of feathers, which are very complicated objects; reform of the respiratory system; reform of the skeletal system, with bones becoming porous, hollow, and in many cases fused; reform of the digestive system to allow increased fuel consumption while economizing on weight; reform of the nervous system, especially the brain and the eyeball; construction of bills and beaks; mastery of nest-building; and, finally, acquisition of flight and all the homing capacities. Any one of these components would be hard to visualize, but when all have to go forward together while keeping the organism in operation at all times, the difficulties become overwhelming."

E. J. Ambrose, professor emeritus of cell biology at the University of London, writes that anything intermediate between a reptilian scale and a feather would be useless and so would be eliminated by natural selection. A bird's feather, moreover, develops from a different part of the embryo than that from which the scale of a reptile comes. Ambrose also points out the impossibility of a workable intermediate between a reptile's lung and a bird's, as they function on entirely different principles.

Douglas Dewar, a prominent English ornithologist, had serious reservations about the standard Darwinian story that reptiles developed the ability to fly simply by jumping between branches: "I am unable to believe that were a reptile, generation after generation, to spend 12 hours daily from the Cambrian onward in leaping from tree to tree the result would be the evolution of wings and feathers."

Dewar also pointed out that birds, like mammals, are warm-blooded, while reptiles are not. Why would natural selection, which cannot know in advance the benefits of being a warm-blooded organism, have "built" an organism whose blood has to be maintained at a constant temperature by a large expenditure of energy, requiring a higher quantity of food? Any transitional animal would have been a far less economical machine than the original reptile and thus handicapped in the Darwinian struggle for existence. The eggs of warm-blooded birds, moreover, have to be kept at a constant temperature. "In consequence, in cold and temperate climates, birds have to incubate their eggs, and, in hot, take precautions to prevent them from being baked by the sun. Reptiles are under no such necessity. Incubation makes great demands on the sitting bird and exposes it to dangers which don't bother the reptile."

The difficulties of the reptile-to-bird scenario, such as how scales turned into feathers, might be solved by a study of transitional forms between the two groups in the fossil record. But there are no such fossils. W. E. Stinton writes in *Biology and Comparative Physiology of Birds*: "The origin of birds is largely a matter of deduction. There is no fossil evidence of the stages through which the remarkable change from reptile to bird was achieved."

Archaeopteryx is often put forward as a transitional species between reptile and bird; but that creature, which was about the size of a pigeon, does not solve any of the problems of bird evolution. It was basically a bird, with feathers as perfect as any living specimen. Its affinities with reptiles are largely cosmetic, and, in any event, bird fossils have been discovered in earlier rocks. It is probably more accurate to say that *Archaeopteryx* is an intermediate, rather than transitional, form. A similar case would be the duck-billed platypus, which has a bill like a duck and fur like a mammal, but is not "transitional" between them. (Darwinists often use the word "transitional" when they should say "intermediate," thereby creating the impression that they have filled a gap on their evolutionary charts.)

The reptile-to-bird scenario presents so many difficulties that Gould and Eldredge, two paleontologists who have disturbed the Olympian calm at the High Table of evolutionary discourse, wrote in the journal *Paleobiology* that in thinking about the change of reptiles into birds, "smooth intermediates . . . are almost impossible to construct, even in thought experiments; there is certainly no evidence for them in the fossil record (curious mosaics like *Archaeopteryx* do not count)."

Darwinian Double-Speak

This is an honest, if (for an evolutionist) disheartening, assessment of the problem. But evolutionists are often careful about where they make these statements. *Paleobiology* is a technical journal read by specialists. It often happens that an evolutionist will publish in such journals an article critical of some aspect of Darwinism, and then write the exact opposite in a book intended for the general public. Read the above statement by Gould and Eldredge, and then consider Eldredge's remarks about bird evolution in his popular book *The Monkey Business*: "Anatomists were among the last holdouts against accepting the idea of evolution. . . . Imagining intermediate stages between, say, the front leg of a running reptile and the perfected wing of a bird seemed to them impossible, as it still does to today's creationists. That the problem perhaps reflects more the poverty of human imagination than any real constraint on nature is an answer not congenial to the creationist line of thought."

Apparently, when the order of the day is attacking creationists, Eldredge's "thought experiments" about bird evolution become much easier. In any event, he is wrong: The scientific problem of bird ancestry is about lack of evidence, not imagination. Gould's evolutionary apologetics show a similar pattern: He has attacked the very foundations of Darwinism in his more technical articles, while giving the impression in his best-selling books (and in his testimony at the "Scopes II" trial in Arkansas) that the theory is only in need of a few patches. Both men, in effect, are groping for an alternative to Darwinian selection while trying to preserve the credibility of evolutionary materialism. This is a daunting project, demanding verbal acrobatics that don't always succeed in disguising the contradictions of their position.

The Neck of the Giraffe

The bird-into-reptile scenario is a test case that eludes a strictly Darwinian explanation. There are too many blank spaces for a step-by-step reconstruction to be remotely possible. But what about simpler problems, like the evolution of the giraffe's neck? In the mind of the public, the long neck of the giraffe is a textbook example of Darwinian selection crafting a new organ to help a species survive. In the sixth (and last) edition of the *Origin* Darwin himself dealt with the neck of the giraffe in trying to counter criticisms that his theory did not explain the continued development of rudimentary organs of apparently no use to the animal into mature ones of a high degree of perfection. The giraffe, he wrote, "has its whole frame beautifully adapted for browsing on the higher branches of trees. . . . [So with] the nascent giraffe, the individuals which were the highest browsers and were able during dearths to reach even an inch or two above the others, will often have been preserved . . . whilst the individuals, less favored in the same respects, will have been most liable to perish."

The plausibility of this explanation evaporates on close examination. First, if a long neck is such an evolutionary advantage, why was the giraffe the only quadruped to develop it? And why are female giraffes on average two feet shorter than male giraffes? Female giraffes, as well as young ones of either sex, would presumably be among the "less favored" who perish "during dearths." And while it is true that the long neck of the giraffe is helpful in reaching high foliage, it is also true that giraffes spend more time eating grass and drinking from puddles than they do pulling leaves off trees. Their long forelegs would make ground-grazing impossible without the long neck. So might we not say that the giraffe "evolved" a long neck to compensate for its forelegs? There is no way of knowing which, if either, explanation is correct.

The problem of the giraffe's neck does not end there. A giraffe needs very high blood pressure in order to pump blood up its eight-foot neck. So, there had to be a dramatic transformation of the entire cardiovascular system, including the development of a very strong heart. But this creates an additional problem: When the giraffe lowers its head to drink or eat from the ground, the high pressure of the blood racing to its head could easily burst blood vessels and cause the animal to black out. Accordingly, the giraffe's neck is equipped with a sophisticated network of blood-pressure sensors and controls that activates whenever the giraffe lowers its head. The giraffe's long neck could not have come into existence without this highly complicated support system.

Like any animal, the giraffe is a sophisticated package of adaptations, any one of which could not have evolved without other transformations occurring at the same time. Darwin's explanation of the giraffe's neck isolates that organ from the rest of the animal and so suppresses the true complexity of the problem. His modern disciples, when they make up their adaptive scenarios, also tend to downplay the intricate mutual dependencies within an organism, since these vastly complicate the job of explaining how natural selection can build an animal from scratch. Darwinists also do not explain how genetic mutations, which are small and random, manage these delicate orchestrations. Pierre P. Grasse writes: "The opportune appearance of mutations permitting animals and plants to meet their needs seems hard to believe. Yet the Darwinian theory is even more demanding: a single plant, a single animal would require thousands and thousands of lucky, appropriate events. . . . There is no law against daydreaming, but science must not indulge in it."

Bears into Whales?

Early scientific critics of Darwin's theory raised a related objection to the mechanism of natural selection that has never been satisfactorily answered. The biologist St.

George Mivart, for example, pointed out that incipient organs were likely to be useless and so would not be available for natural selection. How, for example, did the specialized apparatus that allows a mother whale to suckle her young under water, which includes a special cap around the nipple that fits the snout of the young very tightly to prevent it from taking in water, slowly evolve in the whale's terrestrial ancestors? All modifications would have had to take place before the first whale could successfully suckle her young under water. Why would natural selection bring about such changes in a land mammal?

Darwin's account of the evolution of the whale (which presents many other problems) in the first edition of the *Origin* gives a fair idea of why many scientists felt that he was assuming far more than he was explaining: "I can see no difficulty in a race of bears being rendered, by natural selection, more and more aquatic in their habits, with larger and larger mouths, till a creature was produced as monstrous as a whale."

Darwin seems to have concluded later that there might be more complications in turning a land mammal into a whale than he had supposed, because he quietly deleted this passage from later editions of the *Origin*.

Games Insects Play

The phenomenon of mimicry presents similar problems. Nature is full of look-alikes. There are insects that look like sticks, edible butterflies whose wings look like those of inedible ones, harmless snakes that look like poisonous ones, and so forth. Darwinists plausibly maintain that natural selection evolved these fortunate traits for the good of the imitators. The problem, however, is that the earlier forms are missing. If you were to ask a Darwinist, "What did the Viceroy

butterfly look like before natural selection decided it would
be a good idea for it to mimic the inedible Monarch?" he
would not have an answer.

An insect imitating a leaf, moreover, has to develop a
whole panoply of traits — it has to be flat, oval, green, veined,
and so forth — before it looks like a leaf. Any one of these
changes by itself would make the insect look more, and not
less, conspicuous — which prompts the question of why each
stage would be chosen by natural selection. The famous Darwinist Sir Julian Huxley interpreted the coloring of grass-
hoppers as a camouflage without stopping to consider that
these insects give away their location by chirping.

The Problem of Coevolution

Coevolution is one of the toughest tests for Darwin's
theory because the probabilities seem even more remote.
Throughout nature there are numerous examples of reciproc-
ity between animals, or between plants and animals, that are
so finely calibrated as to make the blind, hit-and-miss process of natural selection seem a grossly inadequate mechanism for their origin.

Take, for example, a species of sea slug that has on its
back brilliantly colored papillae armed with groups of stinging cells. These cells explode in the mouth of a predator,
thereby sending it off with no intention of returning. Marine
biologists studying this curious mechanism were amazed to
discover that these cells do not originate in the sea slug. They
come from the coelenterates (a kind of gelatinous marine
animal) on which the sea slug feeds. The sea slug apparently
can devour the coelenterates without exploding the poisonous cells. As one naturalist writes, "This would seem to be a
kind of miracle, for the nematocysts [explosive cells] are so
conditioned that they explode at the least touch. The touch

of the sea slug is by no means delicate, for, after the habit of all slugs and snails, the harsh, sawlike radula tears its food; yet this violence does not explode the highly explosive sting-ing-cells."

But this is only the beginning of the story. The coelenter-ate, unexploded cells and all, is swallowed by the slug and passes down to its stomach, where the tissues of the coelenter-ate are digested — but not the explosive cells. These are gath-ered into narrow ciliated channels, and are swept up by the workings of the cilia into tiny pouches that lie near the pe-riphery of the papillae. There they are arranged in symmetri-cal rows in such a way that they will discharge against any predator that comes along.

Darwinists assert that such remarkable adaptations originate in the fortuitous coordination of random genetic mutations. The formation of a very simple new structure might depend on five mutations. How likely is this? Most mutations are harmful, and geneticists tell us that maybe one in a thousand is not. The probability of two successful mutations, then, is one in a million. The odds of five are one in one thousand million million (or a quadrillion). And this would be only for one simple organ. The evolution of such complexities as the poison-darted sea slug involves improb-abilities of a much greater magnitude.

Playing the Darwinian Odds

How do Darwinists deal with these impossible odds? The response of Sir Gavin de Beer, a famous twentieth-century evolutionist, to those who invoke against Darwinian selec-tion its "mathematical improbability" is a classic instance of circular argument. Such critics, de Beer writes, "can be re-futed out of their own mouths. Muller has estimated that . . . the percentage of mutations . . . necessary to convert an amoeba into a horse . . . would be on the order of one thousand raised to the power of one million. This impossible and meaningless figure serves to illustrate the power of natural selection in collecting favorable mutations . . . for horses do exist and they have evolved."

In other words, since Darwinian evolution is true, then objections raised about insuperable mathematical odds are by definition invalid. They don't have to be dealt with. Ronald A. Fisher, another prominent Darwinist, writes that natural selection is an agency for "generating an exceedingly high degree of improbability." For Darwinists like Fisher, the strength of natural selection is measured by the enormous odds it overcomes. Ernst Mayr in his influential *Systematics and the Origin of Species* (1942) writes of the inherent improbability of Darwinian evolution: ". . . it is a considerable strain on one's credulity to assume that finely balanced systems such as certain sense organs (the eye of vertebrates, or the bird's feather) could be improved by random mutations. . . . However, objectors to random mutations have so far been unable to advance any alternative explanation that was supported by substantial evidence."

Mayr's strategy for defending Darwin's theory amounts to saying: "I know the claims we make for natural selection seem highly improbable, but since other materialistic explanations of evolution don't work, Darwinism must be true. And since it is true, a Darwinist need not address a problem that common sense would suppose to be a severe challenge to his theory: its extreme mathematical improbability."

Other Problems with the Theory

Darwinism, in sum, seems unable to explain mutual adaptations and the continued development of rudimentary organs into highly specialized ones. This problem of accounting for transitional forms (which, again, are never found in the fossils) would seem to invalidate the theory on terms set by Darwin himself in the *Origin*: "If it could be demonstrated that any complex organ existed which could not possibly have been formed by numerous, successive, slight modifications, my theory would absolutely break down."

There are other problems with classical Darwinian theory, among them the fact that scientists do not always see a "struggle for survival" in nature. Many species tend to co-operate and occupy ecological niches that do not compete. Predators will actually stop preying on another animal group if the numbers of the latter get too low. And there is sex. Asexual reproduction is highly efficient and allows an organism to create a precise copy of itself, something devoutly to be wished by a "selfish" gene. Why did genes — which are allowed no foresight and so could not aim for the advantages of hybrid vigor — devise a costly and complicated process like sex? John Maynard Smith understates the problem when he writes that sex "is something of an anomaly for an orthodox Darwinist. . . ."

Orthodox Darwinists like Maynard Smith, however, seldom admit such difficulties. When confronted with such wonders as coevolution or the exquisite adaptations of almost any plant or animal, they will repeat the phrase "Natural selection, natural selection" like a mantra. In effect, they are following the lead of Charles Darwin, who called the *Origin of Species* "one long argument" that natural selection can accomplish anything if given enough time. We shall now turn to the *Origin* and examine that argument.

Chapter Four

Darwin's "One Long Argument": Does It Hold Up in Court?

"We must not forget how very great an advantage Mr. Darwin has. He has devised a theory according to which any possible utility in any organ is enough to account for its formation." — St. George Jackson Mivart

The Newton of Biology

The *Origin of Species* is, ironically, not about that subject. As Samuel Butler, an early gadfly, put it, Darwin gave us the origin of species with the origin left out. The theory simply explained how already existing species might change into new ones through the agency of natural selection. Darwin admitted to a correspondent after the first edition that he could not point to a single indisputable case of this happening: "You put very well and fairly that I can in no one instance explain the course of modification in any particular instance." His case was entirely theoretical; it was, as he put it, "one long argument," resting on a train of thought rather than empirical evidence.

The very first paragraph of the *Origin* is misleading in that it creates the impression that the author's theory rose spontaneously from observed facts: "When on board H.M.S. 'Beagle,' as naturalist, I was much struck with certain facts in the distribution of the inhabitants of South America, and in the geographical relations of the present to past inhabitants of that continent. These facts seemed to me to throw some light on the origin of species — that mystery of mysteries, as it has been called by one of our greatest philosophers. On my return home, it occurred to me, in 1837, that something might perhaps be made out on this question by patiently accumulating and reflecting on all sorts of facts which could possibly have any bearing on it. After five years work I allowed myself to speculate on the subject, and drew up some short notes. . . ."

The "facts" accumulated during the voyage of the *Beagle* signified nothing until Darwin imposed on them a Malthusian template in his London study. Darwin wanted to do for biology what Malthus had done for political economy: explain everything in terms of the machine model of classical Newtonian physics. He did not ask whether physics, which deals with inert matter, is the proper paradigm for biology — or whether the atomism and reductionism of classical physics can have the same explanatory value when applied to living organisms.

The immense appeal of natural selection derives from its Newtonian simplicity. Like the theories of Marx and Freud, it gratifies the modern passion for explanations that are simple, reductive, and automatic. Its wide acceptance was virtually preordained, since Darwin was bringing a difficult holdout, biology, into the mechanistic worldview inaugurated by Descartes and given immense prestige by the discoveries of Newton. In Darwinian nature, as in Newton's universe, things are more acted upon than acting; they are driven by external forces, like gravity, rather than humors, vitalistic forces, or an internal principle put there by a Creator.

Depew and Weber write in their history of Darwinism: "In portraying within- and between-species change as occurring through selection pressure in an over-populated, competitive, force-filled Malthusian world, Darwin was *applying the highly prized Newtonian models that Lyell had already applied to geology to the history of life, bringing evolutionary theory, for the first time, into the conceptual orbit of respectable British thinking.* This was done by portraying the world of nature as very like the world as political economists saw it."

What Darwin Wanted to Show

What was it exactly that Darwin set out to demonstrate? Principally, that the origin of species could be explained by natural selection accumulating the small variations that occur in plants and animals. There are, in fact, two inseparable arguments in the *Origin*: First, that evolution has occurred; and, second, that natural selection is its prime agent. But the main issue was natural selection. This is an important point, because many of Darwin's early scientific critics, who were ready to accept the historical reality of evolution, balked at the idea that natural selection could be its primary cause.

Darwin himself helped to create the confusion between "evolution" and his own theory of "modification by means of natural selection" by shifting his argument in the course of the book. Gertrude Himmelfarb writes: "Having opened the *Origin* with the assertion that evolution without natural selection was meaningless, that he meant to confine his argument to natural selection since evolution would naturally follow in its wake, he had then proceeded to reverse the process, citing evidence in favor of evolution to bolster the case for natural selection."

In Darwin's view, what had been unsatisfactory about previous theories of evolution, like Buffon's or Chambers's, was their lack of a coherent mechanism. The great French zoologist Lamarck had supplied one — the inheritance of acquired traits; but Darwin and others rightly considered it inadequate. The purpose of Darwin's book is to persuade the reader that species are produced, not by a Creator, but by the blind, materialistic process of evolution. And this is to be done by showing that natural selection is evolution's primary causal agent. The *Origin* is "one long argument" that evolution has occurred by means of natural selection.

The Semantic Shuffle

Darwin's argument has an appealing surface plausibility. Natural selection is simple, elegant, and mechanical. But how convincing is the *Origin of Species* on closer examination? It failed to get a passing grade from some of the sharper minds of the nineteenth century: John Stuart Mill, John Henry Newman, Nietzsche, Charles Sanders Peirce, and William James — a bipartisan panel of intellectuals if there ever was one. Newman, whose Christian orthodoxy was not bothered by evolution, remarked on the "logical insufficiencies" of Darwin's theory, while Nietzsche in a note entitled *Anti-Darwin* observed: "There are no transitional forms. . . . Every type has limits; beyond these there is no evolution. . . . That the higher organizations should have evolved out of the lower has not been demonstrated in a single case. . . . I do not see how accidental variation offers an advantage." Mill, Peirce, and James agreed that the *Origin* did not really prove its case.

Darwin begins by looking at the experience of animal breeders. He makes a clear, if obvious, case for the reality of "variation under domestication." Breeders work on the premise that species are changeable. Darwin gives the example of the pigeon, of which he himself was a fancier. The diversity of pigeon breeds, he writes, "is something astonishing." After detailing the differences between the carrier, short-faced tumbler, pouter, turbit, Jacobin, fantail, and barb, Darwin produces his first trump: ". . . I am fully convinced that the common opinion of naturalists is correct, namely, that all have descended from the rock-pigeon. . . ." And he adds, "Breeders habitually speak of an animal's organization as something quite plastic, which they can model as they please."

After establishing the plasticity of species under domestication, Darwin turns to nature in Chapter Two. Clearly, in nature, varieties also appear. He gives the example of the primrose and the cowslip. These plants differ considerably in appearance, yet a case can be made that "they descend from common parents, and consequently must be ranked as varieties." Darwin now takes a leap that is more semantic than anything else: He asserts that since there can be no firm rule for distinguishing between a strongly marked "variety" and a full-blown "species," then it is not implausible to regard "varieties" as incipient species — or as separate species altogether. Once you concede that "species" and "variety" are virtually the same thing — that the difference in labels is meaningless — then you may admit that new species are as easily generated as varieties. If you concede this, then you may go a step further and admit that, at least in some cases, the origin of "species" (the semantic shift is now in place) is not a supernatural event. Rather, it is a case of descendants varying from their ancestral stock enough to be labeled a new species. What seems to the Christian to be "special creation" is really the result of a purely natural process.

Three comments need to be made at this point.

First, the term "species" is a human invention. What we are really dealing with are genetic packages of astonishing resilience and flexibility. Whether we wish to label these genetic packages "species" or "varieties," the fact is that they all have barriers beyond which they will not go. Darwin's manipulation of the words "variety" and "species" conveniently sidesteps this undeniable fact.

Second, Darwin is setting up a theological straw man. The idea of the "special creation" of each narrowly marked species has neither medieval nor patristic authority; it is sectarian and Protestant, having found its most famous expression in Milton's *Paradise Lost*. The traditional Catholic position, while holding God to be the author of all nature, concedes to nature its own unmiraculous workings, which can include the diversification of species. In other words, there is no contradiction between the idea of God the Creator and the idea that all varieties of pigeons derive from an initial stock by means of secondary causes and not divine intervention.

Third, Darwin so far has presented no more than a statement of microevolution. The semantic shuffle notwithstanding, he has supplied only a description of variation, not a theory of evolution. And if he had stopped there, the first printing of the *Origin* would have sold mainly to pigeon fanciers with a tolerance for reading about what they already knew.

But it is at this point that Darwin makes his radical claim: The micro-changes we see in breeding pens and in nature can be extrapolated indefinitely so as to explain the origin of all life-forms. Once you demolish the immutability of species on the micro-level, Darwin argues, you have demolished it at every level. He staked everything on the idea that, given enough time, species have a virtually unlimited potential to change into something new, and that over the course of time some simple early life-form had diversified into the incredible array of plants and animals we see today.

Does Micro Equal Macro?

Darwin's whole theory rests on this extrapolation of macro- from micro-changes, of evolution from variation. But extrapolation, as any statistician will tell you, is a dangerous procedure. The question is: Was Darwin's extrapolation of macroevolution from these "micro" changes warranted? At this point the reader may logically ask Darwin for concrete examples of the small changes we see within a species adding up to real evolution. Has such a process actually been seen to produce a new animal group? Or even a new organ? But Darwin has no such evidence. After reading the *Origin* with more care than most of his contemporaries, the geologist Charles Lyell wrote to Darwin that the book was "an effective and preliminary statement, which will admit, *even before your detailed proofs appear*, of some occasional useful exemplifications. . . . I mean that, when, as I fully expect, a new edition is soon called for, *you may here and there insert an actual case. . . .*" (Italics mine.)

Lyell was correct: After establishing what breeders had known for thousands of years — that species can subdivide into varieties — Darwin provides no concrete examples of what he really wishes to prove: that "evolution" is this process of variation writ large. His case from this point on depends on speculation rather than hard evidence. Despite his own protestations, he no longer follows the Baconian model of inductive reasoning from the facts; rather, he relies on inventive thinking. Gertrude Himmelfarb writes that Darwin's method in the *Origin* "was neither observing nor the more prosaic mode of scientific reasoning, but a peculiarly imaginative, inventive mode of argument" in which "possibilities are promoted into probabilities, and probabilities into certainties."

Manipulating Tautologies

Darwin proposed natural selection as the mechanism whereby small variations are gradually turned into big evolutionary jumps. It was his task to prove that natural selection can do this; what he did, though, was to use it as an *a priori* explanation for the origin of complex organisms. This circularity is for the most part camouflaged, although he occasionally slips into locutions like, "In living bodies variation will cause the slight alterations. . . . " The mechanism itself — "natural selection, or the survival of the fittest" — has been dismissed by many critics as an empty tautology rather than a testable scientific theory. Jacques Barzun, writing many years ago, was not the first or the last to point out that the idea of the survival of the fittest is entirely circular. Who survives? The fittest. How do we know they are the fittest? They survive. This is like the character in Molière who says that opium causes sleep because of its "dormitive powers."

It is an obvious truism that the "fittest" survive and that plants and animals are "adapted" to their environment. As Hilaire Belloc put it, science did not need Darwin to tell it that if there is a flood the cows will drown and the fish survive. The question is whether the "struggle for survival" is the mechanism whereby one animal group changes into another. C. H. Waddington, one of the major biologists of the twentieth century, dismissed the idea of natural selection as "vacuous," saying that it "merely amounts to the statement that the individuals which leave the most offspring are those which leave the most offspring." The only claim that can be made for natural selection is that it eliminates what doesn't work. Arnold Lunn argued that to call natural selection creative, as many evolutionists do, is a bit like saying that the Nazi air strikes against London during World War II were creative because they left Westminster Abbey standing.

The destruction of the unfit, in other words, does not explain the origin of the fit. Hans Driesch, the famous embryologist, complained that to use natural selection as an explanation of anything is like answering the question "Why does the tree have leaves?" with "Because the gardener did not cut them away." Similarly, you cannot explain the existence of the polar bear by saying that bears of another color could not survive in the polar regions.

The late Karl Popper, universally regarded as a referee of what constitutes a valid scientific theory, complained that Darwinian selection is not, strictly speaking, a scientific theory because it can neither make predictions nor be rigorously tested above the micro-level, where it is a mere truism. Unlike Einstein's theory of gravity, the idea of evolution by natural selection is in principle not falsifiable. No matter what the complexity of an organism, a Darwinist can always make up an "adaptive" story explaining its origin. And when pressed to explain a severe problem, like the usefulness of incipient organs, he can take refuge in the unobservable. This was Darwin's own tactic in later editions of the *Origin*, where he seems chiefly to argue that since the transitional stages of animal groups are hidden, his theory cannot well be refuted.

Fierce protests from the Darwinian camp eventually caused Popper to retract his criticism without explaining why. The retreat was also demanded by Popper's own philosophical materialism. But his point that Darwinism is not a hard science applies to much of the *Origin*. One problem is the glib explanatory power of natural selection, which allows

Darwin to have it both ways when dealing with difficult facts. Are there both winged and wingless beetles on the island of Madeira? Darwin explains in a long and not terribly logical passage why this is to be expected. Are there species that persist without changing for millions of years? They "have a singularly inflexible organization." Are there other species that change? These are cases of "a whole organization seeming to have become plastic, and tending to depart from the parental type."

The problem is that if a theory explains too much it really explains very little. For example: If a scientist were to say that the universe is really a giant computer, he could not, strictly speaking, be refuted. Every event in the universe, including your protest, could be ascribed to the workings of this computer. But while this scientist could not be refuted, he could be safely ignored, because his theory, being neither testable nor scientific, explains nothing. The same is true of natural selection. If a coroner were to write on every death certificate, "Cause of death: He (or she) stopped breathing," he would be making a statement that in a sense is true. But his "explanation" would not be very helpful. Cessation of breath is a necessary condition of the fact to be explained but is not its real cause. This is the case with natural selection. The fact that all species are adapted does not mean that those adaptations fully explain the origin of each species.

Another Darwinian Circle

Another problem for Darwin's theory is the discontinuity found everywhere in nature. Whether one looks at the fossils or at living plants and animals, one finds systematic gaps between major groups. This fact is not "predicted" by Darwin's theory, which insists that evolution is a gradual, step-by-step affair. Why, he asks rhetorically, "if species have descended from other species by fine gradations, do we not everywhere see innumerable transitional forms?"

There was (and is) absolutely no evidence that the barriers between the higher animal and plant groups have ever been crossed by minute gradations. Yet, Darwin was adamant that his theory was dead on arrival unless this was the case. This compelled him to make a circular argument about the "imperfection" of the fossil record: It was imperfect because it did not contain the transitional forms whose existence he was trying to prove. Eldredge writes that Darwin's discussion of the gaps in the geological record "is one long *ad hoc*, special-pleading argument designed to rationalize, to flat-out explain away, the differences between what he saw as logical predictions derived from his theory and the facts of the fossil record."

The Problem of the Eye

There is another logical flaw in Darwin's mode of argument: He repeatedly takes for granted what most of all requires explanation in light of his theory. For example, when dealing with "organs of extreme perfection and complication" such as the eye, whose intricacies make an IBM supercomputer seem low-tech, Darwin starts with a "light-sensitive spot," which certain animals indeed possess, and then adds complexities to complexities and calls that an explanation. He assumes, against large odds and with no factual evidence, that each component appeared in perfect form exactly when needed and in perfect lockstep with the other components: "*I can see no very great difficulty* [a phrase Darwin uses often] . . . in believing that natural selection has converted the simple apparatus of an optic nerve . . . into an optical instrument as perfect as is possessed by any member of the great Articulate class. . . . He who will go thus far . . .

ought not to hesitate to go further, and to admit that a structure even as perfect as the eye of an eagle might be formed by natural selection, although this case does not know any of the transitional grades. *His reason ought to conquer his imagination. . . .*" (Italics mine.)

Darwin asks the reader to accept that a highly implausible chain of events *might* have happened. But this is not proof that it did happen. And if the reader's imagination balks at how a light-sensitive spot orchestrated itself into a fully developed eye — with a movable iris, a focusing device, built-in correction features for chromatic aberrations, and the incredibly intricate connections of nerve cells in the retina that carry out many types of preliminary data-processing of visual information before transmitting it to the brain in binary form — he is told to conquer "imagination" with "reason." In other words, stick to the abstract argument rather than get hung up on "imagining" how these changes were managed. But this is the same Darwin who wrote to Asa Gray that, since there is no hard evidence to support these difficult scenarios, one's "imagination must fill up the very wide blanks."

The eye, whose complexities multiply indefinitely in light of modern molecular biology, is apparently no problem for modern evolutionists, either. In a book whose title, *Macroevolutionary Dynamics*, implies that the reader will learn how the evolution of complex organs like the eye occurred, Niles Eldredge writes the following: "Thus complex 'vertebrate-type' eyes have appeared at least twice in evolutionary history. Pronouncing such transformations as a priori 'impossible' is thus ruled out of court; if we accept the hypothesis that life has evolved, such structures had to be derived from simpler states. Insisting that their complexity speaks against their being evolved reflects, instead, a poverty of imagination than any necessary conclusions drawn from a consideration of complexity of structure per se."

Ernst Mayr of Harvard, dean of modern neo-Darwinists, is similarly unperturbed: "There is no need to postulate rare or unique events, since eyes evolved in the animal kingdom at least 40 times independently." In other words, the evolution of the eye can be explained by — the existence of the eye. Like Darwin, Eldredge and Mayr confuse the observation of a phenomenon with its explanation. Much Darwinian literature depends on this sleight-of-hand logic. But to repeat: The adaptation of a species to an environment does not explain the origin of that adaptation. John Stuart Mill was rightly suspicious of the Darwinist habit of citing purposes as explanations.

The God of the Galápagos

Darwin makes use of one final argument when both reason and imagination seem to falter. It is one whose truth is necessarily assumed in the above statements about the eye. You hear it in many forms when you press Darwinists about the shortcomings of the theory; they get testy and respond with something like: "There is no God, therefore it *had* to be that way." But this is theology, not science. Darwinists, in fact, are as guilty as their creationist adversaries of violating the boundary between science and religion. The *Origin* itself is full of God-talk. Darwin apparently imagined God to be like an Anglican bishop, and since the carnage and waste he saw in places like the Galápagos could not be the work of such a being, he adduced the mechanism of natural selection as the only alternative. In later writings, like the *Variation of Animals and Plants* (1868), Darwin is quite blunt: We have to choose between a Creator and natural selection, and since a Creator would be responsible for many inexplicable things, ranging from the occurrence of vestigial organs to the Lisbon earthquake, then evolution by natural selection must be true.

This crude theological reasoning occurs repeatedly in the *Origin*. It can be reduced to a syllogism: The Divine Watchmaker of Anglican theology does not exist; therefore natural selection is the cause of adaptation, and the more extraordinary the adaptation, the greater the glory of natural selection. On page after page of the *Origin*, Darwin places in opposition to his theory a Creator who does not seem to know what he is doing. On page 55 of the original edition we read that "if we look at each species as a special act of creation, there is no apparent reason why more varieties should occur in a group having many species, than in one having few." On page 394 the Creator is taken to task for not putting mammals (except bats) on volcanic islands. And on page 406 we read that the variations of animals on colonized islands are "utterly inexplicable on the ordinary view of the independent creation of each species. . . ."

Darwin, in other words, rules out of court a God who allows all the messy contingencies we observe in nature. Similarly, Gould likes to point to the odd engineering of the panda's thumb as showing that nature cannot be the work of "a sensible God." What Gould is really demonstrating is that theology is outside the professional competence of a Harvard paleontologist.

Science *ought* to explain things without reference to a Creator. But Darwin went further: His arguments are full of theological postulates that do not belong in a work of science. Like Marx and Freud, he let his views about God slip in the back door at night and passed it off as science in the daylight. And his theology was amateurish. It really amounted to the haphazard thoughts of a Whig gentleman about the

Anglican Watchmaker. They are not to be compared to anything found in the works of Augustine or Aquinas.

Darwin's Flexible Strategy

Darwin was acutely aware that the edifice he had constructed was entirely theoretical. His claim was, not that natural selection had actually been seen to create new species, but that in theory it *could* create them. The abstract argument is studded with facts; but most of these facts show only that variation occurs within species and that the similarities of structures between animal groups point to the possibility of common descent. In fact, the real accomplishment of the *Origin* was to make plausible the idea that such descent had occurred. Regarding his main point, natural selection, he left open a line of retreat of which he took full advantage in later editions. C. D. Darlington, an enthusiastic evolutionist, writes that Darwin "engaged in a flexible strategy which is not to be reconciled with even average intellectual integrity." Mayr, who has boundless admiration for Darwin, admits, "On almost any subject he dealt with — and this includes almost all of his own theories — he not infrequently reversed himself."

Darwin's many twists and turns set the pattern for the subsequent history of his theory of evolution, to which we now turn.

Chapter Five

Ashes to Ashes: Darwinism Since Darwin

The Reception of the Origin of Species

No book has so profoundly affected the way modern man views himself than the *Origin of Species*. And yet, the book's argument that evolution is the result of natural selection failed to persuade the audience that Charles Darwin most cared about: the leading scientists and philosophers of Victorian England. Among scientists, only Alfred Russell Wallace, the codiscoverer of the theory, thought that Darwin had satisfactorily explained the origin of species. And it must have been galling to Darwin that England's three leading philosophers of science — Whewell, Herschel, and Mill — were unconvinced. The majority of biologists who accepted evolution after 1859 remained skeptical about natural selection. They thought that Darwin had made a strong case for evolution but had not adequately demonstrated how it had occurred.

Darwin's vociferous "bulldog," Thomas Henry Huxley, was a typical case. His views about the scientific merits of the theory might politely be described as ambiguous. Although his public posture was "Darwinism or nothing," he believed that the theory lacked proof and that Darwin's insistence on gradualism was not supported by the fossil record. In 1887, five years after Darwin's death, he admitted that no amount of artificial breeding had produced a new species and that the theory consequently rested on an "insecurity of logical foundation."

69

Huxley championed Darwin because Darwin was an evolutionist, and not because he believed the theory of natural selection. For progressives of Huxley's generation, evolution was an assault weapon to be used against the religious and political establishment they despised. The ideological relish with which he and other intellectuals embraced Darwin had little to do with the scientific validity of his theory. What mattered was the "truth" of evolutionary materialism; the serious technical problems of Darwin's mechanism were almost beside the point.

In reviews and private correspondence, scientists like Lyell and Hooker questioned the extravagant claims that Darwin made for natural selection. Darwin himself was increasingly plagued by doubts after the first edition of the *Origin*. In subsequent editions, he kept backing off from natural selection as the explanation for all natural phenomena. Loren Eiseley writes in *Darwin's Century* that a "close examination of the last edition of the *Origin* reveals that in attempting on scattered pages to meet the objections being launched against his theory the much-laboured-upon volume had become contradictory. . . . The last repairs to the *Origin* reveal . . . how very shaky Darwin's theoretical structure had become." Darwin's unproved theory nonetheless had become dogma in the public mind.

Science Versus Darwin

Yet, there was sharp scientific opposition from the start. As Swedish biologist Soren Lovtrup points out, most of Darwin's early opponents, even when they had religious motives, "argued on a completely scientific basis." In fact, in the decades following Darwin's death in 1882, his theory came increasingly under a cloud. Lovtrup writes that "during the first third of our century, biologists did not believe in Darwinism. . . ." Hans Driesch in Germany, Lucien Cuenot in France, Douglas Dewar in England, Vernon Kellogg and T. H. Morgan in America, biologists and geneticists with international reputations, all rejected Darwin's theory during this period. Cuenot wrote that "we must wholly abandon the Darwinian hypothesis," while the *Dictionaire Encyclopedique des Sciences* in 1925 (the year of the Scopes trial) dismissed Darwin's theory as "a fiction, a poetical accumulation of probabilities without proof, and of attractive explanations without demonstrations."

The Scopes Trial

The great irony is that the Scopes trial in 1925, which the American popular imagination still regards as putting to rest the whole case against Darwin, took place against this background of general dissent. The story is still celebrated in song and myth. In 1925 the Tennessee legislature passed a statute outlawing the teaching of Darwin's theory. Although the governor on signing the bill pronounced it a dead letter, the ACLU, then as now acting as the legal arm of secular humanism, persuaded a substitute biology teacher in Dayton to press the case. The scientific issues were never properly discussed in the courtroom. The director of the American Museum of Natural History went on radio to promote a fossil tooth, the remains of something called "Nebraska Man," which later turned out to belong to a pig. And William Jennings Bryan made the mistake of allowing his fundamentalist beliefs to be ridiculed on the witness stand by Clarence Darrow, who was a kind of Village Atheist raised to the national level.

The Scopes trial proved nothing about the scientific validity of Darwin's theory, but it did establish in the American mind the notion that in the debate over evolution one

must choose between the beliefs of Bible-thumping fundamentalists and those of Darwin. G. K. Chesterton remarked
at the time that the Catholic Church, which does not have a
philosophical problem with evolution (properly understood)
and does not treat the Book of Genesis as a sourcebook of
scientific data, was entirely outside the fray.

Anti-Darwinian Evolutionists

By the end of the 1920s, evolutionary theory was a frag-
mentary collection of postulates and theories that did not
hang together. The most significant developments in twentieth-century biology — the rediscovery of Mendel's papers on
inheritance in 1900 and the subsequent laboratory work of
geneticists like T. H. Morgan — were not viewed as supporting Darwin. The leading Mendelians in the first third of this
century — Bateson, de Vries, and Johannsen — rejected natural selection as the cause of evolution. They ascribed evolutionary change to sudden and undirected mutations in genes
(a view that has its own problems). In countries like France
and Russia, there was no need to reject or reevaluate Darwin
because he had never been accepted by a majority of biologists in the first place. The Russians never bought Darwin
because they had never bought Malthus. Russia was vast and
underpopulated, and its intelligentsia could not make sense
of the English idea that selection pressures produce novelties.

In the Anglo-Saxon countries, where most scientists
at least agreed on the importance of promoting evolutionary materialism, geneticists and paleontologists were barely
on speaking terms. G. G. Simpson's description in *Tempo
and Mode in Evolution* (1944) of the situation between the
two disciplines during this period has a certain charm and
validity even today: "Not long ago paleontologists felt that

a geneticist was a person who shut himself in a room, pulled down the shades, watched small flies disporting themselves in milk bottles, and thought that he was studying nature. . . . On the other hand, the geneticists said that paleontology had no further contributions to make to biology. . . . The paleontologist, they believed, is like a man who undertakes to study the principles of the internal combustion engine by standing on a street corner and watching the motor cars whiz by."

The Rise of Neo-Darwinism

It was not until the early thirties that the evolutionary establishment began to agree on enough issues to allow the emergence of the so-called synthetic theory, or neo-Darwinism. The Synthesis incorporated genetics, molecular biology, and complicated mathematical models. But it remained completely Darwinian in its identification of random variations preserved by natural selection as the driving force of evolution. Julian Huxley, the chief spokesman for the synthetic theory, claimed that Darwinism had "risen Phoenix-like from the ashes." Historian Peter Bowler makes a more telling point when he claims that Darwin's theory did not really "triumph" until the Synthesis was in place seventy years after the publication of the *Origin*.

The founding document of the Synthesis was Sir Ronald Fisher's *The Genetical Theory of Natural Selection* (1930). Fisher, a mathematical prodigy, believed that statistical models of genetic changes within local populations explain all of evolution. He and his disciples were not much interested in actual animals. Their focus was the mathematics of changing gene pools. As Lovtrup points out, Fisher's confidence in the supremacy of mathematics had an interesting consequence: He appeared to believe that his mathematical formulas constituted empirical evidence for evolution. More-over, like all neo-Darwinists, Fisher made two tacit and highly questionable assumptions: that within-population variation can be extrapolated across the board into major evolutionary change; and that natural selection *must* be the agency that directs this change.

Fisher, in fact, was guilty of a logical fallacy when he argued that once you eliminate all known alternate theories (Lamarckism and so forth), then natural selection *must* be true: "The sole surviving theory is that of Natural Selection, and it would appear impossible to avoid the conclusion that if any evolutionary phenomenon appears to be inexplicable on this theory, it must be accepted at present merely as one of the facts which in the current state of knowledge does seem inexplicable."

Lovtrup comments on this passage: "Fisher does not exactly state that if empirical facts do not agree with his theory, then the facts must be false. But he is not very far from this point, and he certainly seems to have raised a shield protect-ing the theory from any attempts at falsification."

The Synthesis, which is still the model of evolution taught in college textbooks, assumes that evolution can be explained by changes in gene frequencies, by the accumu-lation of small genetic substitutions. It is both strongly re-ductionist — the genes are studied in isolation from each other and the organism — and strongly selectionist: Natu-ral selection is *the* cause of all natural phenomena. Even Darwin did not go this far in the *Origin*. And when it comes to demonstrating that natural selection has actually pro-duced the dramatic diversity among plants and animals, the proponents of the Synthesis rely more on abstract analo-gies than empirical evidence. When they do scan nature for instances of selection in action, the cases they find merely demonstrate variation, not evolution; these cases may even be said to show the opposite of what Darwinists wish to demonstrate.

The famous textbook case of natural selection is Kettlewell's observations of "industrial melanism" in the peppered moth. When trees in a certain part of England were blackened by industrial smoke, dark-colored (melanic) moths became abundant because predators had difficulty seeing them against the trees. When the trees became lighter because of reduced pollution, light-colored moths again became abundant. This case, however, does not seem to prove anything beyond Belloc's axiom about the differential survival of cows and pigs after a flood. There were dark and light moths from the start; only their relative numbers changed for obvious reasons. And the ability to produce both light- and dark-winged varieties would seem to *preserve* a particular species of moth under these conditions rather than change it into something else. If anything, the example demonstrates the stability of species rather than the transformational power of "selection pressures."

For decades, the geneticists, and not naturalists or zoologists, dominated the field of evolutionary biology. The talk was all about genetic machinery. The problem with this phase of Darwinism was that the phenomenon that had to be explained was the change in *forms* and not gene frequencies. Contradictory fossil evidence was ignored or explained away, while the difficult problems of animal morphology dissolved into soothing phraseology. Are transitional forms a problem? Not really. Species, according to neo-Darwinists, go through "nonadaptive" and "preadaptive" phases. Are there puzzles that even natural selection seems unable to explain? Again, no problem. There is "genetic drift." Evolution was assumed to be an accumulation of small genetic copying errors, whose permutations were expressed by mathematical models intelligible only to a small minority of biologists.

The Decline of Neo-Darwinism

But as C. H. Waddington, one of the major biologists of the century, complained, "The whole real guts of evolution — which is how do you come to have horses and tigers and things — is outside mathematical theory; you are still left with the vacuous explanation of natural selection." Genetics and molecular biology turned out to be no help, either. In *Evolution: A Theory in Crisis* (1986), molecular biologist Michael Denton demolishes the idea that natural selection could have produced at random the smallest elements of life — the functional protein or gene. And "to get a cell by chance would require at least one hundred functional proteins to appear simultaneously in one place," which is outside the realm of probability. A cell is so complex, writes Denton, that it exceeds "anything produced by the intelligence of man." It is also irreducible; a simpler "ur-cell" would not work. So how, asks Denton, could cells have randomly "evolved"? It would be like a volcano spewing out a factory.

Biochemist Michael Behe makes a similar argument in *Darwin's Black Box* (1996). As a biologist, Behe is struck by the incredible intricacy of the molecular machines that power the cell. These machines have finely calibrated parts, the absence of any one of which would disable them. How can Darwinism explain the exact cascade of chemicals that must be triggered in order for blood to clot? It can't; because if you remove a single link in the process, it won't work. Any precursor to the blood-clotting mechanism would be nonfunctional and therefore would not be chosen by natural selection. In other words, there's no gradual Dar-

winian route between these mechanisms and whatever preceded them.

Molecules and Life

Below the level of gross anatomy, then, the problem of
how evolution occurs has become more, and not less, acute.
Everything we know about DNA points to the fact that it programs a species to remain what it is, and that large mutations are invariably lethal. Darwinists do not really answer
the question of how single random beneficial mutations,
which alone are highly improbable, can accumulate in an
organized manner to bring about genuine evolutionary novelties. Grasse compares mutations to "a typing error in copying a text," adding that they "in time, occur incoherently.
They are not complementary to one another, nor are they
cumulative in successive generations toward a given direction."

There is also the problem of explaining the origin of life
and of genetic coding. In the late fifties, Stanley Miller, a
graduate student at the University of Chicago, caused enormous excitement when he created a few amino acids by spark-
ing with electricity a closed flask containing water, methane,
and hydrogen. But since then the quest to create life in a
laboratory tube has made no progress and has been quietly
abandoned by many scientists. So far as we know, life only
seems to come from life. And even if someday a scientist were
able to accomplish the seemingly impossible task of creating
from inert chemicals a biologically functioning protein, it
would still not prove a materialist scenario for the origin of
life, because it would be human intelligence that produced
it.

As for the origin of genetic coding, we should perhaps
give Darwinian theory a "bye" on explaining how DNA, a

strand of which contains more organized information than the *Encyclopedia Britannica*, assembled itself from random nucleic acids that happened to be in the neighborhood. Science is still at the beginning of a steep learning curve in understanding how DNA operates. But there remains a question for geneticists: They know that DNA programs a species to remain what it is; but do they know what genes do when one species turns into another? Have they ever observed "speciation" on the genetic level? Richard Lewontin of Harvard, the dean of American geneticists, would probably describe himself as a Darwinist. But he writes in his influential book, *The Genetic Basis of Evolutionary Change* (1974), that "we know nothing about the genetic changes that occur in species formation." And again: "It is an irony of evolutionary genetics that, although it is a fusion of Mendelism and Darwinism, it has made no direct contribution to what Darwin obviously saw as the fundamental problem: the origin of species."

Ernst Mayr writes that he does not know precisely how the "genetic revolutions" on which his version of evolution depends are accomplished. He simply infers that they *must* happen. In other words, geneticists, like paleontologists, do not see the crucial episodes of an evolutionary process that they assume to be true.

The Death of Neo-Darwinism

In 1980 Stephen Jay Gould, who plays both pope and Luther in the debate over Darwin, published a notorious essay entitled "Is a new and general theory of evolution emerging?" This inaugurated a genre of science writing whose purpose is to preserve Darwinian materialism while finding a replacement for Darwinian selection. Recent contributions include Eldredge's *Reinventing Darwin* (1995) and numerous books and articles about "complexity" that Behe and others criticize as "fact-free" science. The point, though, is that Gould in that essay echoed the private sentiments of many scientists when he declared, "The synthetic theory . . . is effectively dead, despite its persistence as textbook orthodoxy." But since the synthetic theory originally arose in response to the collapse of classical Darwinism at the turn of the century, where does that leave scientists today?

Evolution by Jerks

"Punctuated equilibrium," would be the reply of most biology teachers and popular-science columnists. This is the theory that Gould and Eldredge came up with in the early seventies to deal with the obvious shortcomings of neo-Darwinism. They deserve credit for finally taking the gaps in the fossil record seriously, although their solution to the "gap" problem could be construed as an attempt to shelter Darwinism from empirical falsification. According to the "punk eek" scenario, small groups of animals break off from the herd, migrate to peripheral locations "at the edge of ecological tolerance," and mutate rapidly into something like "hopeful monsters" who return to replace the old herd. Because the changes occur so quickly, geologically speaking, there is no fossil evidence. Scientists once said that macroevolution is so slow that we cannot see it; now the punctuationists tell us that it is too fast.

Gould and Eldredge admit that there is no direct evidence that evolution occurred this way — in rapid speciation "events" among small groups. The evidence is strictly negative. Eldredge writes that "the actual evidence for periods of rapid evolution lies in the *absence* of . . . intermediate organisms." In fact, their hypothesis can be viewed as an *ad hoc* attempt to cope with the collapse of Darwinian gradualism. And plenty of scientists do not buy the "evolution by jerks" scenario, pointing out, among other problems, that it lacks a mechanism. How, for example, did the bat suddenly find itself with a workable sonar? True or not, punctuated equilibrium is really a *refutation* of Darwin, who said that his theory would break down completely "if it could be demonstrated that any complex organ existed, which could not possibly have been formed by numerous, successive, slight variations."

Other Schools of Thought

Besides the punctuationist camp, there are two other evolutionary schools of thought today. First, there are those who cling to classical Darwinism because they say there is no better explanation for the origin of species. For these scientists the engine of species creation is small DNA-copying errors that add up over millions of years to the plethora of life-forms we see today. They cheerfully admit the mathematical improbability of their scenarios (the odds of the evolution of a single-celled organism has been calculated as virtually zero by Jacques Monod), but rest their case on the fact that it did happen. Historical description is thus called upon to perform the duty of explanation. It is the faith of these retro-Darwinists that, given enough time, anything can happen — and did.

Then there are those scientists who think that the mystery of the origin of species is unsolved and that Darwinian selection, which predicts what amounts to a truism (the survival of those most likely to survive) rates no more than a footnote in biology textbooks. Skepticism about Darwin is more widespread among scientists than is genuinely supposed. In 1984, a group of anti-Darwinian scientists weighed in with a technical volume called *Beyond Neo-Darwinism*, in which two American biologists, Gareth Nelson and Ron Platnick, wrote, "We believe that Darwinism . . . is, in short, a theory that has been put to the test and found false."

The late Pierre P. Grasse, perhaps the most eminent zoologist of his generation — he was president of the French Academy of scientists and editor of the twenty-eight volumes of the *Traite de Zoologie* — wrote that Darwinism is "either in conflict with reality or cannot solve the basic problems." Grasse's indictment is severe; he argues that "through the use of hidden postulates, of bold, often unfounded extrapolations, a pseudo-science has been created. It is taking root in the very heart of biology and is leading astray many biochemists and biologists, who sincerely believe that the accuracy of its fundamental concepts has been demonstrated, which is not the case."

Micro Does Not Equal Macro

Like Gould, Eldredge, Stanley, and others, Grasse argues forcibly that macroevolution must be "decoupled" from microevolution. In other words, the phenomena that evolutionists have spent most of this century observing and tallying — the frolics of fruit flies in bottles or the variation of birds on islands — is of no relevance to the question "Where do the higher animal groups come from?" These scientists reject extrapolation and, with it, the argument of the *Origin of Species*. This has put Gould in a delicate situation, since he wishes to champion Darwin as the master thinker of evolutionary materialism *and* to attack scientists who actually believe Darwin's theory, whom he labels "ultra-Darwinists." When Gould says that he favors "pluralism" in evolutionary theory, what he really means is that he wants to have it both ways: Keep Darwin as an icon, but dispense with the core of his theory. This explains the muddled thinking in his widely read books and articles. Richard Dawkins, one of Gould's "ultra-Darwinist" adversaries, once began an article with a priceless sentence that applies to Dawkins himself: "If only Stephen Jay Gould thought as clearly as he writes."

Evolutionary Agnostics

Serious scientists like Grasse, who have no interest in these propaganda wars, call themselves "evolutionists" because they recognize that all life-forms share basic characteristics such as DNA and so may be descended from a single ancestor; but they are frankly agnostic about how this happened. One of these agnostics, a biologist at the American Museum of Natural History, summed up to me the situation of evolutionary theory today: "We know that species reproduce and that there are different species now than there were a hundred million years ago. Everything else is propaganda."

Darwinism today is in a severe crisis. And yet it remains the ruling paradigm in biology. What will change this situation? Thomas Kuhn, in *The Structure of Scientific Revolutions*, perhaps the most influential book written in the sixties, argues that change from one scientific paradigm to another is more a matter of conversion than proof. Scientists will cling to a theory despite falsifying evidence until a new explanatory framework shakes up their old assumptions. When scientists change their mind about interpretative frameworks they simply see the evidence differently. At present, Darwinists do not wish to think differently. But if history is any guide, their theory will eventually go the way of Ptolemy's astronomy — not without wailing and gnashing of teeth.

What is lost, scientifically speaking, if Darwin is finally shelved in the museum of discarded paradigms? Not much, really. Biologists and molecular biologists can go on publishing research papers, which seldom refer to evolution. Paleontologists can dig up more bones and fit them into hierarchical schemes that would look pretty much the same if Darwin had never written a word. Geneticists can still zap fruit flies with X rays and watch them mutate into — fruit flies. As for Darwin's zealous disciples: The philosopher A. N. Whitehead once remarked that their devotion to the purpose of proving there is no purpose "constitutes an interesting subject for study." They will increasingly be viewed as promoting an Anglo-Saxon faith system, the last offshoot of nominalism, planted like a foreign body in the heart of biology.

Chapter Six

"I Love Lucy": The Question of Human Origins

"When considering our origins it is clear that we have often been less than objective." — Richard Leakey

"I have come to believe that many statements we make about the hows and whys of human evolution say as much about us, the paleontologists and the larger society in which we live, as about anything that 'really' happened." — David Pilbeam

The Hominid Gang

The search for human origins fascinates the modern public. Whenever a so-called hominid skull or tooth is discovered in places like east Africa, the engines of modern publicity kick into high gear. First, there is the carefully timed disclosure in scientific journals like *Nature.* Then there are press conferences and solemn rearrangements of man's family tree on the nightly news broadcasts. On the rare occasions when these shreds of bone are exhibited in museum halls, they command the sort of hushed reverence once accorded to the relics of saints. They are even the subject of biographies, which caused Chesterton to quip that people talk of Pithecanthropus as though he were Pitt or Napoleon.

The paleontologists who dig up these fossils also become instant celebrities. As the discoverers of Skull 1470 and "Lucy," respectively, Richard Leakey and Donald Johanson possess an aura that makes other members of their profession look like stamp collectors. A significant hominid find in Kenya or Ethiopia is paleontology's rough equivalent of going triple platinum or winning the grand slam in golf. As a result, no area of science is so skewed by ferocious personal rivalries.

Darwin, who was allergic to controversy, devoted just one sentence of the *Origin* to the topic of human ancestry. In the course of investigating the earth's fossil history, he surmised, "Light will be thrown on the origin of man and his history." But he expected his readers to draw the desired conclusion: Man, like dogs and pigeons, had evolved in a gradual, mechanistic fashion from more primitive species. The most celebrated and acrimonious exchange to follow the publication of the *Origin*, the debate between Huxley and Bishop Wilberforce in June 1860, brought the issue wide into the open. In his usual bulldog fashion, Huxley went on to write a book entitled *Evidence as to Man's Place in Nature* (1863). Man's place, he concluded, was among the primates, and he looked at the fossils to see what they showed about our descent from some apelike creature.

The problem that confronted Huxley (and Darwin when he came to write the *Descent of Man*, published in 1871) was that there were precious few fossils to go on. A few Neanderthal bones comprised the entire inventory of possible hominid remains. (The word "hominid" denotes the earliest humans and their putative ancestors.) Huxley thought that, since the Neanderthal skullcap had contained a modern-sized brain, it could not be regarded as the remains of "a human being intermediate between Men and Apes." So, at the time when the Darwinian ape-to-man scenario was shaking the moral foundations of Europe, there were no fossils even hinting at man's descent from earlier primates. This, of course, did not stop ardent evolutionists like Ernst Haeckel from publishing elaborate family trees, giving man's undiscovered ancestor a local habitation (Africa) and a name (*Pithecanthropus alalus*).

Bones of Contention

Then, in 1891, a young Dutchman named Eugene Dubois found in the East Indies a skullcap, some teeth, and a femur that ultimately came to be known as "Java Man." The bones were scattered over some forty-five feet and probably did not belong to the same creature. When Dubois returned to Europe to announce the discovery of this "missing link" he also failed to mention that he had found in nearby deposits bones that definitely belonged to modern humans. Some scientists immediately rejected Java Man, saying that all Dubois had found was a gibbon's skull and a human leg-bone. Late in life Dubois, who for decades allowed no one to see the specimens, also came to have doubts. Nonetheless, he had supplied the "missing link" demanded by Darwin's theory, and his Java Man was quickly embraced by Haeckel and others eager to fill in man's evolutionary blanks.

Thus began the assembly of that small collection of bones that today pass for hominid remains. They have received more scrutiny than any objects in history. The search for new ones involves relatively few players, all of who behave as though in a high-stakes poker game. These rivalries have a marked effect on the interpretation of what is dug up. There is, in fact, a history of the experts seeing in "hominid" fossils exactly what they want to see. Hypotheses arise unbidden by the evidence, and are quietly shelved when some new bone is unearthed or dating method challenged. The evidence itself is sparse. Richard Leakey quotes fellow paleontologist David Pilbeam: "If you brought in a smart scientist from another discipline and showed him the meager evidence we've got, he'd surely say, Forget it, there isn't enough to go on."

Darwinists who wish to read man's ancestry into the available fossils face several problems. First, in the words of Richard Lewin, they have to explain "how causes operating through nature have in the case of *Homo sapiens* produced an effect that is radically unlike anything else in nature." In the *Descent* Darwin tried to argue that the difference between ape and man was one of degree and not of kind. He asserted that the gulf could be bridged by small, purely quantitative changes. But more than a few scientists, then and now, do not find this argument convincing. The difference between man and the most "advanced" chimp is neither small nor purely quantitative.

Champions of the Darwinian view of human origins also have to deal with the gaps-in-the-record problem. The fossils do not show gradual, progressive evolution. Hominid species like *Australopithecus afarensis* ("Lucy") appear fully formed in the fossil record and change very little until they disappear. The apparent sudden jumps in the hominid line were initially attributed to the incompleteness of the record. Find enough fossils, the argument went, and a smooth, linear progression from ape to man would be revealed. But as more bones were dug up, the opposite occurred. Pilbeam writes: "It is now clear that [human] evolution is much more like a bush than a ladder. You simply cannot draw long lines through time as we were doing."

Bushes and Ladders, Again

Pilbeam's point is that early candidates for our fossil ancestors, like Lucy, may or may not be in that category. In trying to determine their status, the experts face a twofold problem: There is a marked discontinuity between species; and the pattern of their appearance is more like the twigs of a very complicated bush than a simple line running up a central tree trunk. There is no way of knowing whether Lucy is on the trunk leading directly to the top branch of *Homo sapiens* or whether she represents an evolutionary dead-end — a mere twig, so to speak. Did *Australopithecus afarensis* give rise both to *Australopithecus africanus* and *Homo sapiens*? Again, we don't know. There is no clean line linking man and these early apes. As a result, honest paleontologists have been reduced to saying the following: There was once a hypothetical ancestor of both man and apes that lived between five million and eight million years ago, and the line of descent from this creature to *Homo sapiens* seems to have passed through a bewildering maze of intermediates that may never be sorted out.

As a result, the connect-the-dot charts of human evolution found in high-school textbooks are misleading. They belie the fact that there is no simple linear progression from early apes to man that paleontologists can agree on. The two most famous figures in hominid paleontology today, Richard Leakey and Donald Johanson, are in complete disagreement about man's ancestry. *Australopithecus afarensis* has been rendered in textbooks with faces ranging from purely ape to human, depending on whose side the artist is on. In fact, during the past half-century, man's ancestry has changed as often as the weather, as the small collection of hominid bones has been shuffled about by the experts. Sometimes, a "missing link" — Piltdown Man, Nebraska

Man, *ramapithecus* — is loudly publicized, only to be subsequently retired.

Richard Lewontin, professor of zoology and genetics at Harvard, gives a blunt assessment of where the search for man's antecedents stands today: "We don't know anything about the ancestors of the human species. . . . Despite the excited and optimistic claims that have been made by some paleontologists, no fossil hominid species can be established as our direct ancestor."

The Dating Game

Another seldom-discussed problem of hominid paleontology is what might be called the dating game. Radioactive dating uses minerals like uranium (decaying into lead) and potassium (decaying into argon). Since the radioactive-decay rates for these minerals are normally uniform, scientists measure the proportion of, say, potassium/argon in a rock sample and then conclude that the rock is so many millions of years old.

But radioactive dating depends on several unverifiable assumptions: First, that the minerals were in the rocks for millions of years without any contamination, leaching, or mixing. Second, that radioactive-decay rates never vary; but they will vary if, for example, the mineral is exposed to the sort of intense cosmic radiation that visits the earth now and then. Another problem is that we cannot know the initial ratios of, say, potassium/argon in a sample rock; in fact, as much as one percent of the earth's atmosphere consists of argon, and rocks can easily absorb this gas. So how is one to know how much of the isotope argon 40 has come by decay from potassium and how much from the atmosphere?

Some of these problems have been partially solved by

the use of newer dating methods like electron-spin resonance. There are good reasons to accept the earth's age of 4.5 billion years and the dating of geological markers such as the Cambrian and Cretaceous. But nailing down the dates of recent (geologically speaking) hominid bones is still a tricky business. The skeleton might have been buried among rocks more ancient than itself, for example, or mixed with stone tools of a later date. And, in fact, the dating of hominid fossils has been changed when subsequent discoveries have made the original dating inconvenient, the most notorious case being that of Richard Leakey's Skull 1470.

From Lucy to Laptops

The attempt to impose on the fossils an evolutionary "story" leading to man depends, in the words of British anthropologist Lord Zuckerman, "partly on guesswork, and partly on some preconceived conception of the course of hominid evolution." As is the case with all animal groups, the crucial branching point where the human line supposedly split off from that leading to modern apes is shrouded in mystery. Researchers believe that the last common ancestor of humans, chimpanzees, and gorillas lived in Africa between five million and eight million years ago, but this creature has never been found. Lewontin and Zihlman write: "Imaginations run riot in conjuring up an image of our most ancient ancestor — the creature that gave rise to both apes and humans. This ancestor is not apparent in ape or human anatomy nor in the fossil record."

Several million years after this hypothetical ancestor, the fossil record produces its first visible hominid candidate: the australopithecines, or "southern apes." The first, the "Taung child," was discovered in South Africa in 1924 by Raymond Dart. The most famous member of the group,

"Lucy" (*Australopithecus afarensis*), is a three-and-a-half-foot skeleton found by Donald Johanson in Ethiopia in 1974. This creature, dated at 3.2 million years ago, was clearly not human. It had a small brain and may or may not have walked upright. Regarding Lucy and her set, Pilbeam writes: "We have no grounds for thinking that there was anything distinctly human about australopithecine ecology and behavior. . . . The australopithecines are rapidly sinking back to the status of peculiarly specialized apes." Such a verdict did not stop the curators of New York's Museum of Natural History from placing in its Hall of Human Evolution a diorama showing a pair of australopithecines, contemporaries of Lucy, as protohumans out for a walk on the east African plains, apparently discussing a serious abstract matter while strolling home for dinner.

After the australopithecines, the genus *Homo* appears suddenly on the charts in the form of *Homo habilis*. This is a much-contested category. Some experts claim that it is no more than a taxonomic parking space for the odd assortment of bones that dates from roughly 2.2 million to 1.6 million years ago. Some of these specimens are probably australopithecines; others, like Skull 1470, probably human. There is also a chronological problem, because 1.6 million years ago, when the youngest *Homo habilis* populations supposedly lived near Mount Kilimanjaro, *Homo erectus* was already walking on the shores of Lake Turkana in northern Kenya. The australopithecines may also have been still around.

This tendency of hominid species to overlap one another in the fossil record makes it very difficult to construct a chart of human evolution. "What has become of our ladder [to *Homo sapiens*]," writes Gould, "if we must recognize three coexisting lineages of hominids (*A. africanus*, the robust australopithecines, and *Homo habilis*), none clearly derived from the other? Moreover, none of the three display any evolutionary trends during their tenure on earth: none become brainier or more erect as they approach the present day."

In light of these facts, paleontologist Steven Stanley writes: "The old idea of *Australopithecus africanus* being gradually transformed into *Homo erectus* by way of *Homo habilis* is now difficult to defend. The slender australopithecine may conceivably have turned into '*Homo*' *habilis*, but the abrupt appearance and subsequent stability of the more distinctive *Homo erectus* are suggestive of punctuational [i.e., abrupt] transition to this younger species."

Leaving *Homo habilis*, we move up the chart to *Homo erectus*, who, paleontologists believe, evolved into modern man. But he may simply have been an early member of the human family. There is no clear break between *Homo erectus* and *Homo sapiens*, merely a microevolutionary continuum. *Homo erectus* had a pronounced brow and more sloping forehead than we do, but his brain size reached up to twelve hundred cubic centimeters, which is within the range of modern man. He was living in Australia, moreover, at a time when *Homo sapiens* was already on the scene. So, *Homo erectus* may have been an early race of man, differing little more from us than modern races can differ from one another. The same is true of Neanderthal man. Recent molecular evidence that modern humans are not descended from this race, which was abruptly replaced by Cro-Magnon man forty thousand years ago, does not mean that they were not human cousins — just as the fact that no living Watusi tribesman is descended from an Eskimo does not mean that both are not full members of the human family. The archaeological remains of the Neanderthal give every indication that they possessed a recognizably human culture.

Mind Out of Matter?

No matter where we place the taxonomic marker that divides man from the other primates, the most striking feature of the fossil record is the explosively fast growth of the hominid brain from species to species. Gould writes: "Our brain has increased much more rapidly than any prediction based on compensations for body size would allow." The big leaps in brain size over relatively short periods in the fossil record point to a problem that Darwinists have not succeeded in explaining even to the satisfaction of fellow materialists. This is the problem of the human mind. While the fossils and comparative anatomy suggest that we are biologically related to the rest of the animal kingdom, the extraordinary capabilities of the human mind also suggest an enormous abyss that Darwinists cannot easily bridge.

Paleolithic paintings and other remains indicate the suddenness with which man's unique mental attributes appear on the scene. Reviewing this evidence, Chesterton, who had no problem with the hypothesis of evolution, observed: "Monkeys did not begin pictures and men finish them. Pithecanthropus did not draw a reindeer badly and Homo sapiens draw it well. . . . The wild horse was not an Impressionist and the race-horse a Post-Impressionist. . . . There is not a shadow of evidence that this thing evolved at all. There is not a particle of proof that this transition came slowly, or even that it came naturally. . . ." Man, in other words, differs in kind and not just degree from other animals.

Darwin claimed that the emergence of man's special attributes — will, intelligence, artistic creativity — can be explained by the incremental workings of natural selection. But this claim does not square with his insistence that natural selection "tends only to make each organic being as perfect as, or slightly more perfect than, the other inhabitants" of an ecological niche. Alfred Russell Wallace, the codiscoverer of evolution via natural selection, was not alone in thinking that the human mind could not be explained in this way. Natural selection, he wrote, "could only have endowed a savage with a brain little superior to that of an ape, whereas he actually possesses one but very little inferior to that of the average members of our learned societies."

Some modern evolutionists agree with Russell that science may be incapable of explaining the human intellect. Bernard Campbell writes in an otherwise orthodox Darwinian book, *Human Evolution: An Introduction to Man's Adaptations*, that "it is not easy to account for the capacities of the human brain if it is seen as merely the product of a hunting and gathering life-style." Monkeys have no apparent need for greater intelligence, and it is also obvious that humankind did not need the capacity to write *Hamlet* or compose *Don Giovanni* in order to win a Darwinian competition with other species. What makes us special is neither predicted nor required by Darwin's theory.

Man is endowed with attributes no ape even begins to possess. You have free will and a conscience. You have language and art-making abilities. Apes do not. You could spend years trying to explain to the "smartest" chimpanzee what the Super Bowl is, or the difference between Democrats and Republicans, and the chimp would reward you with a blank gaze. Teams of scientists have spent hundreds of thousands of dollars trying to get chimps to communicate in a human fashion. But chimps cannot be trained to use or understand syntactic rules. Moreover, for a chimp, signs and symbols are merely means of getting what he wants; they are not used to convey any other information. Learning for a chimp means being trained or conditioned to behave in a certain way; it does not mean understanding reasons or causes.

The ability to use language is a "quantum leap" that cannot be readily explained by a Darwinian process. It is difficult to account for even the physical basis of language, since, according to Noam Chomsky, special neuronal-integrating circuits had to exist in the brain before sentences could be spoken. Lord Zuckerman, the famous anthropologist and a materialist who believes that man is descended from apes, writes that "there is nothing with which to compare language. However it came about, there is no form of animal vocalization with which it can be functionally compared. Language exists sui generis. That is why we are what we are. And that is a mystery no less profound than is the origin of life itself."

Darwinism's inability to explain basic human realities such as mind, purpose, and ethics would seem to acutely embarrass its scientific credentials. If man is simply an ape taken a few degrees higher, then the history of man from Paleolithic times onward should be explainable in Darwinian terms. While it is obviously true that people and societies compete and occasionally try to eradicate one another, there has never been a society that bears any resemblance to the Darwinian model of ruthless struggle. Life was certainly not like that in Victorian England. In fact, there would be no history at all if man's tendency to cooperate did not far outweigh his competitive instincts. Philosophers who insist that people always behave in a Darwinian manner are, in the words of philosopher David Stove, simply indulging in "some sufficiently silly *a priori* anthropology." Even man's more perverse and destructive activities seem to disconfirm Darwin's theory. Take, for example, the practice of abortion. As Darwin wrote: ". . . the instincts of the lower animals are never so perverted as to lead them regularly to destroy their own offspring. . . ."

Evolutionary materialism's dealings with man reveal

another major flaw that is never seriously acknowledged by its proponents. If man is no more than an accidental colla-tion of atoms, a purely contingent product of blind material forces, then humans do not possess a free will. If this is so, we cannot trust any products of the human intellect, includ-ing books by Darwinists. This is the Achilles' heel of all mate-rialist philosophies; their truth claims are self-canceling be-cause they downgrade human consciousness to an epiphe-nomenon of matter. Novelist Walker Percy's sly remark that the *Origin of Species* explains everything except Darwin writ-ing the *Origin of Species* neatly summarizes the problem.

Gene Machines

Humans, according to Darwinian reductionists like Dawkins and E. O. Wilson, are simply machines for DNA to make more DNA. Dawkins writes that "we are . . . robot-ve-hicles blindly programmed to preserve the selfish molecules known as genes." Dawkins's own DNA apparently decided that the way to accomplish this was to have him write *The Selfish Gene.* The calculation must have been that the book's popu-lar success would give him more opportunities to mate. I don't know whether this has turned out to be true. But if Dawkins and Wilson are correct that people are no more than disposable biological matter concocted by their genetic cod-ing for its own ends, then his indignation at those who dis-agree with him is hardly consistent. His critics are also pris-oners of a mechanistic process, and they should not be held responsible for the gene-driven motions of their brains. Their DNA molecules have apparently decided that one ticket to replication is to have their human hosts disagree with Dawkins.

A week spent pondering the philosophizing of scien-tists like Dawkins and Wilson will persuade most sensible people that the retirement of Darwin's theory in the sphere of science can only improve the intellectual tone of neighboring disciplines like sociology and ethics. It will have no effect on literature and art, however, because since the time of Darwin no great writer or artist has paid any attention to his theory. Imagine if Tolstoy or Proust had believed that we are blindly programmed "robot-vehicles." The best they could have done was to write early versions of cyber-fiction, populating their books with automatons rather than individuals who are free to make interesting choices.

Darwinism, with its elimination of contours, distinctions, and essences, cannot begin to cope with the phenomenon of man. Even the fossil record, which loosely educated people believe to show a smooth cascade from some lemurlike creature to man, reveals profound discontinuities between us and the rest of the animal kingdom. Far from rubbing our edges away, science accentuates them. And so does common sense, if it is allowed to operate free of materialist ideologies.

Chapter Seven

Planet of the Apes: Darwinism as a Modern Ideology

"We take the side of science in spite of the patent absurdity of some of its constructs, in spite of its failure to fulfill many of its extravagant promises of health and life, in spite of the tolerance of the scientific community for unsubstantiated just-so stories, because we have a prior commitment, a commitment to materialism." — Richard Lewontin

The Flight from Metaphysics

Since the Enlightenment, Western man has been engaged in a flight from metaphysical truth. Metaphysics deals with ultimate questions, such as the nature of being (ontology) or the origin of the universe (cosmology). A major solvent of metaphysical truth was the work of Descartes and Kant. Both thought that one could not ask basic questions about reality until one answered the question "How do I know what I know?" Ontology was thus preempted by epistemology, and Western philosophy found itself in the odd situation of an eyeball trying to examine itself. Bedrock metaphysical concepts like causality were jettisoned, and educated people were no longer bothered by the traditional (and still valid) proofs of the existence of a Creator — or, at least, of an Aristotelian Prime Mover.

The flight from metaphysics was aided by the apotheosis of the scientific method, which began with Francis Bacon. The great ancients Plato and Aristotle never dreamed that the natural sciences could usurp the role of wisdom. But this is what has happened. For centuries we have thought that major philosophical questions have "scientific" answers. We have forgotten that while science can give us valuable quantitative statements about material reality, it is incapable of explaining that reality. It is not within the competence of the scientific method to discuss the origin of the universe — to explain, that is, why there is something rather than nothing. But modern man will not accept answers to such questions that do not come in a scientific package. This absolutizing of the scientific method has hurt both science *and* philosophy. As Stanley Jaki puts it, once you treat science as the key to reality, it "becomes perverted into a gnosis, and philosophy becomes a ghost." Scientists who do philosophy under the guise of science corrupt both science and philosophy.

With Darwin, Western man's trashing of metaphysics was complete. If man is no more than a random whirl of atoms, the product of a mindless process indifferent about its results, then it is pointless to ask the large metaphysical questions "Why are we here?" "Where are we going?" Or, for that matter, "Why should we adhere to a code of ethics?" John Dewey wrote approvingly in 1920 that after Darwin, "philosophy forswears inquiry after absolute origins and absolute finalities." Dewey, working in the tradition of American pragmatism, was interested in what works and not in what is true. Pragmatism remains America's philosophical norm. It has created a society where "things get done" with the help of wonderful gadgets — and this is not to be lightly dismissed. But it is a society that hasn't quite grown up, because the truly important questions are swept to the periphery.

Marx Reads Darwin

Apart from pragmatism, Darwinism fed into the Promethean revolt against God that gathered force in the nineteenth century. Incorrigibly Anglo-Saxon by temperament, Darwin was not interested in the role of cosmic rebel. Atheistic intellectuals on the Continent, however, did not share this inhibition. These intellectuals were waiting for a "scientific" excuse for their rejection of God, and the publication of the *Origin of Species* exactly fit their purpose.

Karl Marx, for example, badly needed Darwin's theory. In an early manuscript written fifteen years prior to the *Origin,* he asserted that man cannot rightfully proclaim to be his own master if he owes his existence to something other than himself. He admitted that the idea that man has no external cause makes no sense. People, after all, cannot create themselves. But he found the notion of man as a contingent being intolerable. How did he deal with this problem? He prohibited its discussion. The question of man's origins, he wrote in a memorable sentence, "is forbidden to socialist man."

Darwin's book solved Marx's dilemma. Man, it turned out, was the result of a blind, mechanistic process that operated very much like dialectical materialism. Marx was so delighted that he wanted to dedicate a volume of *Das Kapital* (1867) to his English mentor. Darwin, who had no desire to involve himself in politics, declined. It is scarcely possible to exaggerate the subsequent influence of Darwin's theory on Marxist thought — and therefore on the crimes committed, and still to be committed, by Marxist regimes. Lenin wrote in *State and Revolution* (1917) that Marxism is simply Darwin applied to politics. The *Origin* was also among the forbidden books passed around the Russian Orthodox seminary attended by the young Stalin, who, like Hitler, became an apostate Christian.

Rockefeller Reads Darwin

Paradoxically, Darwin also had an unsavory influence on the development of capitalism. The founding document of capitalist thought, Adam Smith's *Wealth of Nations* (1776), took for granted a traditional ethical grounding for economic behavior. Capitalism, in Smith's view, did not mean ruthless competition with no moral restraints. Economic activity was to be conducted within a framework governed by natural law. But many capitalists in the late nineteenth and early twentieth centuries preferred Darwin's view of things. The idea of the universal struggle for existence gave the robber barons "scientific" license for predatory behavior. "The growth of a large business," declared John D. Rockefeller (in a Sunday school address!), "is merely survival of the fittest. This is not an evil tendency in business. It is merely the working-out of a law of nature and a law of God." Andrew Carnegie also believed that the laws of economic competition had strictly biological foundations. "I remember," he wrote in his autobiography, "that light came as in a flood and all was clear. Not only had I got rid of theology and the supernatural, but I had found the truth of evolution."

Hitler Reads Darwin

It was in Germany that Darwin had the most traumatic influence. The generals who launched World War I were quite open about using his ideas as a rationalization for their warmaking. While it is simplistic to say that Darwin's theory was the cause of World War I, the generals' behavior nonetheless illustrates Dostoyevsky's dictum that ideas have consequences. George Bernard Shaw in his preface to *Heartbreak House* (1919) wrote: "We [Anglo-Saxons] taught Prussia this religion; and Prussia bettered our instruction so effectively that we presently found ourselves confronted with the necessity of destroying Prussia to prevent Prussia from destroying us." Adolf Hitler also found Darwin useful. He said, for example, that "if we did not respect the law of nature, imposing our will by the right of the stronger, a day would come when wild animals would again devour us. . . . By means of the struggle the elites are continually renewed. The law of selection justifies this incessant struggle by allowing the survival of the fittest. Christianity is a rebellion against natural law, a protest against nature."

Nazism was fed by another intellectual current flowing from the work of Darwin (and his mentor, Malthus): eugenics. Darwin's cousin, Francis Galton, was its modern founder. The purpose of eugenics is to multiply the "fit" while reducing the number of "unfit." In his private correspondence, Darwin, quite logically in light of his theory, expressed approval of the extermination of various aboriginal races deemed inferior to Europeans. Today, the international population movement, whose most cherished goal is to reduce "surplus population" in the Third World (curiously, these activists never regard *themselves* as surplus population) wages a cultural imperialism quite Darwinian at its core. Yet, here we find another paradox: The popularity of contraceptives in affluent societies flatly contradicts Darwin's statement in the *Origin* that "every single organic being around us may be said to be striving to the utmost to increase in numbers."

Darwinism in the hands of many twentieth-century thinkers is an ideology masquerading as science. The thrust of that ideology, whether appropriated by the left or right, is to reduce man to matter. And if scientists and philosophers are going to do that, if they are going to treat man as no more than disposable biological material, then that is exactly what he will be. It is a short step from Darwin to the gas ovens and abortion mills. In the minds of their founders, the most reprehensible ideologies of this century were "scientifically" grounded in Darwin's ideas.

Street Darwinism

Apart from giving "scientific" license to dangerous ideologies across the political spectrum, Darwinism has saturated the moral and intellectual atmosphere inhaled by the average citizen of the late twentieth century. It is not a doctrine about which he thinks rigorously or consistently. To use philosopher David Stove's arresting distinction, when it comes to Darwinism, there are Hard Men and Soft Men. The Hard Men — Marxists, Nazis, eugenicists — don't fudge their Darwin. They regard man as a thing and behave accordingly in the political sphere. But there are also the Soft Men, who comprise most of the educated public.

The Soft Man, Stove writes, "is intellectually at ease. Having been to college, he believes all the right things: that Darwin was basically right, that Darwin bridged the gap between man and animals, etc., etc. He also believes, since he is not a lunatic, that there are such things as hospitals, welfare programs, priesthoods, and so on. But the mutual inconsistency of these two sets of beliefs never bothers him, or even occurs to him. He does not think that his Darwinism imposes *any* unpleasant intellectual demands on him. . . . Still less does he think that his Darwinism requires him to advocate eugenics, or to oppose welfare programs, as the Hard Men do. In fact, the politics of Darwinian Hard Men fill the Soft Man with horror. They do, at any rate, until the suburb where he lives is taken over by blacks, or Shi'ite Moslems, or Croats, or Sikhs, or whatever."

These street Darwinians nonetheless dimly share the Hard Man's Darwinian anthropology. If pressed about the nature of man, they would say that man does not possess an unchanging essence. If pressed further, they would admit that, since this is so, there are no unchanging norms governing human behavior. Instead of locating moral truths, post-Darwinian man must invent them. Morality is a matter of convenience, not metaphysical necessity. This is one of the most disturbing consequences of Darwin's anthropology. It rid Western man of the idea that he possesses an unchanging nature that makes him fundamentally different from brute animals.

The fixity of species, including man, had been a given of Western thought since the ancient Greeks. A corollary was the existence of constant metaphysical norms governing man's existence. These norms were considered to be beyond whim and manipulation. They were expressed in the Ten Commandments, the Hippocratic oath, and the great theological synthesis of the Middle Ages. Chesterton wrote that post-Darwinian man was not so much bothered at seeing his forefathers in the zoo, as by the vision of man as a "shifting and alterable thing." The highest scientific authorities now told him that not only did he not possess a dignity that exceeded anything in creation but that he was an accidental product of purely material laws, inhabiting a meaningless vortex of atoms called the universe.

This meaningless vortex has been a valuable piece of real estate for certain artists and intellectuals, who are only too pleased to further the education of our Soft Man on the street. The free-floating nihilism that informs much of contemporary art would not have been possible without Darwin.

The novelist Salman Rushdie, who delights in mocking all forms of religion, told *Newsweek* magazine in 1990: "I am a modern, and a modernist, accepting uncertainty as the only constant, change as the only sure thing. I believe in no god — I have spiritual needs, but I am content to try and satisfy those needs without recourse to any idea of a Prime Mover or ultimate arbiter." There we have post-Darwinian man in a nutshell.

If change is the only "sure thing," as Darwin's disciples assure us, then there are no fixed norms for human behavior. But most Darwinists feel they have to draw the line somewhere. Even nihilism, as Saul Bellow observes, has its no-no's. But no amount of intellectual gymnastics can disguise the fact that evolutionary materialism is a frontal assault on morality. If I firmly believe that I and the universe are a random flux of atoms serving no purpose, then I have a choice between sentimentalism and nihilism. I cannot claim that my restraint in not shooting a person who annoys me has anything to do with objective morality. The same goes for sexual behavior. Aldous Huxley wrote in 1937 that one reason he and other intellectuals of his generation had embraced modernism was that it gave them a license for unlimited sex. The first name he mentioned was Darwin. If man is no more than a trousered ape, then the logical Darwinian thing to do is behave like an animal.

Thomas Henry Huxley, in some respects a typical High Victorian, was disturbed by the moral implications of evolutionary materialism. Like Darwin, he was a combination of Hard Man and Soft Man. He nevertheless resisted attempts to extract a moral code from Darwin's theory. While there may be an "evolution of ethics," he wrote, "there cannot possibly be an ethics of evolution." This thought has not registered with the legions of Darwinian humanists, including most academics, who see no contradiction between their insistence on absolute norms when fighting racism and sexism and their belief in Darwin.

Darwinism Versus Religion

If they thought about it, secular humanists would not be comfortable with Darwinism's denial of the metaphysical common sense found in works ranging from Plato's *Dialogues* to Martin Luther King's "Letter from the Birmingham Jail." Darwinism's antagonism to religious faith is another matter, however. In fact, the tenacity of Darwin's theory among scientists and educators in the face of so much negative evidence can be explained by the fact that it is a very effective club with which to beat religion. Richard Dawkins, Darwin's modern attack dog, is typical of this class of thinker when he writes that religion is a "virus" that "infects people's minds, replicates and spreads." He ridicules scientists who profess a belief in God and claims that the great merit of Darwinism is that it allows one to be "an intellectually fulfilled atheist."

Evolutionary materialists like Dawkins relish the corrosive effects of Darwinism on organized religion. These scientists *a priori* will not accept any possibility that evolution is not blindly random at its core, because such a possibility would give aid and comfort to people who believe in God. For them, philosophical materialism *precedes* scientific thinking. That is why Karl Popper called Darwinism "a metaphysical research program." Popper urged that the main effort of a scientist ought to be to try to falsify his theory in order to make room for a better one. Darwinists do the opposite. Since their theory is the scientific prop of their materialism, they spend most of their intellectual energy finding ways out of predicaments, concocting *ad hoc* explanations, and playing semantic games. Darwinism, in fact, is metaphysical in the worst sense of the word.

Darwinism as Religion

Popper's critique points to another irony: Darwinism itself has become a kind of religion. In their determination to rid nature of a Creator, Darwin's modern disciples show every sign of being under the sway of a dogma to which they wish to convert the rest of mankind. There is deep evangelical fervor in their writings. They are on a mission to disabuse the public of what G. G. Simpson, a founder of neo-Darwinism, called "the higher superstitions celebrated weekly in every hamlet of the United States." Evolutionists like Simpson and Dawkins are quite candid about their contempt for Christianity, which can burst out at any moment, even during a discussion of trilobites. Others, like Gould, are more careful. They adopt a more subtle (and effective) strategy against religious faith.

Gould, for example, will write in his popular column in *Natural History* magazine that there is no real conflict between religion and science, so nobody has to worry. But by "religion" he means strictly a system of ethics. It is nice that people want to behave well. Gould endorses good behavior. But almost everything he says touching on man is meant to promote a fierce counter-metaphysics that is irreconcilable with any religion other than secular humanism. He writes, for example, that all we have to do is give up an "antiquated" concept of the soul in order to embrace our unity with the rest of nature. Gould's implicit strategy is to dollop out nice homeopathic doses of philosophical materialism — strong enough to accomplish his purpose but not so strong as to compromise his cozy panda-bear image on public television.

When their antagonism toward religion is brought to

their attention, Darwinists often respond that it is their duty to exclude design (and hence a Designer) from their scientific thinking. Simpson writes that "the progress of knowledge rigidly requires that no non-physical postulate ever be admitted in connection with the study of physical phenomena. . . . The researcher who is seeking explanations must seek physical explanations only. . . ." If Simpson is saying that it is not the business of a scientist to seek supernatural explanations, he is correct. But he is really making a larger claim: that phenomena have only material causes, and therefore only scientific explanations. Like Marx prohibiting the question of human origins, Simpson is saying that intelligent people should not raise even the possibility that behind the proximate causes investigated by science there may be other causes that admit only of metaphysical inquiry.

What Simpson is doing is surreptitiously promoting a valid methodological principle (we scientists deal only with secondary causes) to the status of a metaphysical dogma (there is no First Cause). It is an inadmissible leap of logic. But secular faith systems like Darwinism rely on these intellectual shell games. By rigorously excluding divine causality at the beginning, Darwinian theory guarantees that it will not appear at any other point of the discussion. Evolutionary materialism, in Lewontin's words, must be "absolute, for we cannot allow a Divine Foot in the door."

Darwinism in the hands of scientists like Simpson and Lewontin is really a religion in reverse. It exhibits all the features normally associated with religious faith: missionary zeal, the anathematizing of heretics, the handing down of dogmatic pronouncements by a magisterium of "experts." And there is catechesis for young people. This often takes the form of classroom videos. The biology teacher, with a solemn air of neutrality, tells his eighth-grade class that they are about to hear two sides of an important debate about which they are free to make up their own minds. The lights go down, the VCR blinks, and the children watch a preacher with slightly crazed features explain how the earth was created six thousand years ago and that evolutionary theory is bunk. The camera then switches to an attractive scientist wearing a white smock. She is standing in a laboratory. She calmly explains how all life-forms, including man, are descended via natural selection from some simple organic form floating in the primordial soup billions of years ago. The lights come up. Boys and girls, which side are you on?

Around 1959, the centenary year of the publication of the *Origin*, when neo-Darwinian triumphalism was at its height, a very astute philosopher named Marjorie Grene wrote an essay entitled "The Faith of Darwinists." She observed that all the Darwinian books she had read violated a rule of logic by assuming the truth of what they were claiming to prove. And she was struck at how the theory of evolution can seem so certain to the Darwinian faithful, while being so obviously flawed to a philosopher on the outside like herself. Little has changed in the past forty years. In fact, with the collapse of Marx and Freud, the intellectual establishment now clings to Darwinism with even greater fervor. It is their creation myth. And it is not clear how it will finally be retired.

Christians who try to make their peace with Darwin ought to examine their metaphysics. Did God intend from all eternity that man exist in his present form? If the answer is yes, then Darwinism in its pure philosophical state is inadmissible. Many Christian thinkers are in a muddle about this. On the one hand, they accept Darwin's story that we are the result of a blind, mechanistic process. On the other hand, they believe that we are created in the image of God. When pressed about the contradiction, they usually get hung up on scientific details. But the real issue is philosophical. There is no contradiction between the existence of a Creator and an evolutionary process that may have some mechanistic features. There is, however, a contradiction between belief in a Creator and the Darwinian idea that we are *solely* the result of a mechanistic process. Both the Magisterium of the Catholic Church and major Catholic thinkers have grasped this essential point. We shall now examine how the Church has dealt with Darwin.

Chapter Eight

Is God a Creationist? The Catholic Church and Evolution

Pope Vindicates Darwin?

On October 22, 1996, Pope John Paul II delivered a message to the Pontifical Academy of Sciences regarding the theory of evolution. The document touched on a number of issues — scriptural, epistemological, and scientific — of supreme importance to Catholics. Inevitably, it was the least newsworthy item in the pope's message — that the Church has no problem with evolution so long as divine causality is not excluded — that produced screaming headlines around the world: "Pope Vindicates Darwin!"

The pope, in fact, did no such thing. Darwin's name was nowhere mentioned in the document, and the pope made it clear that Darwinism in its pure, materialistic form is not acceptable to Catholics. In their coverage of the letter, the *New York Times* and other conduits of misinformation about the Church made the usual mistake of equating "evolution" with Darwin's theory of random mutation and natural selection. But John Paul is aware of the distinction, and he laid down guidelines for dealing with the "theories" of evolution. As he always does when discussing science, he reiterated the Second Vatican Council's insistence that the natural sciences have a legitimate sphere of autonomy that ought to be respected by the Church.

John Paul's letter was not the first time the Magisterium had addressed the issue of evolution. Pope Pius XII had done so in *Humani Generis* (1950). For almost a century prior to that encyclical letter, Darwin's theory had elicited no direct response from the Church. Perhaps recalling the fiasco of the Galileo affair — one of which every two thousand years is enough — the Magisterium had taken a cautious posture toward evolution as a scientific theory. No scientific book about evolution was put on the Index, and Catholic scientists like the English biologist St. George Jackson Mivart were free to engage in evolutionary speculations. Mivart's book *On the Genesis of Species* (1871) became a touchstone on the issue for English-speaking Catholics. While accepting the idea of macroevolution, Mivart mounted a stinging (and still valid) attack on Darwin's mechanism of natural selection. Newman, who saw "nothing in the theory of evolution inconsistent with an Almighty Creator and Protector," commended Mivart for his treatment of the issue.

Early Catholic Response to Darwin

When the *Origin* was published, the first Catholic response appeared in the English Catholic journal *The Rambler* (March 1860). The reviewer took the long philosophical view, calling in the heavy artillery of Aristotle and Aquinas. Wasn't Darwin simply recycling Empedocles's idea that living beings had been formed, not by creation for any final cause, but by a chain of fortuitous accidents? And hadn't that teaching been refuted by Aristotle? The reviewer chided Darwin for implying that the "special creation" of each species was an immemorial Christian doctrine. Neither Augustine nor Aquinas had taught it. Evolution was conformable with orthodox theology. What was objectionable in the *Origin* was its materialistic philosophy. The reviewer also took exception to the theological claims made by Darwin's defenders, principally T. H. Huxley. Even if the theory were proven to be correct about man's physical origin, Huxley had no right to assert that it therefore ruled out "any faith in the spirituality of the soul or the creative action of God."

The great *Catholic Encyclopedia* of 1907 included a long entry on evolution, which is perhaps as close to an "official" Catholic response to Darwin as one can get during this period. The authors of the entry, comprising two articles of several thousand words, were well aware of the widespread scientific skepticism about Darwinian selection. But, like Mivart and Newman, whom they cite, they are accommodating to the idea of evolution: ". . . the theory of evolution as a scientific hypothesis . . . is in perfect agreement with the Christian conception of the universe; for Scripture does not tell us in what form the present species of plants and animals were originally created by God. As early as 1877 Knabenbauer stated 'that there is no objection, so far as faith is concerned, to assuming the descent of all plant and animal species from a few types.' "

The article goes on to discuss the theory's theological implications: "God is the Creator of heaven and earth. If God produced the universe by a single creative act of His will, then its natural development by laws implanted in it by the Creator is to the greater glory of His Divine power and wisdom. St. Thomas says: 'The potency of a cause is the greater, the more remote the effects to which it extends' (*Summa c. Gent.* III, c. lxxvii); and Suarez: 'God does not interfere directly with the natural order, where secondary causes suffice to produce the intended effect' (*De Opere Sex Dierum*, II, c. x, n. 13)."

The article asserts that an atheistic theory of evolution can explain neither the origin of the cosmos nor the law of its development, "since it acknowledges neither creator nor lawgiver." It mentions the possibility of "theistic" evolution, which "postulates an intervention on the part of the Creator in the production of the first organisms," and concludes with an observation that would not have to be reworded today: "When and how the first seeds of life were implanted in matter, we, indeed, do not know. The Christian theory of evolution also demands a creative act for the origin of the human soul, since the soul cannot have its origin in matter. The atheistic theory of evolution, on the contrary, rejects the assumption of a soul separate from matter, and thereby sinks into blank materialism."

On the sensitive subject of human origins, the article eschews what would now be called creationism: "That God should have made use of natural, evolutionary, original causes in the production of man's body, is *per se* not improbable. . . ." But, it adds, the "actual proofs of the descent of man's body from animals is . . . inadequate, especially in respect to paleontology."

Finally, the article makes a distinction that is crucial to a Catholic treatment of the issue: "Darwinism and the theory of evolution are by no means equivalent conceptions." And it points out the central flaw of Darwinism: "As a theory, it is scientifically inadequate, since it does not account for the origin of attributes fitted to the purpose, which must be referred back to the interior, original causes of evolution. . . . As far as facts teach us, new species do not arise by selection."

Pius XII Issues Humani Generis

On August 12, 1950, Pius XII issued *Humani Generis* in order to check certain heterodox trends in Catholic biblical theology. Regarding the theory of evolution, whose materialist version had given rise to "new erroneous philosophies," Pius urged great caution. He correctly pointed out that evolution had not been fully proved, but he did not forbid "that the theory of evolution concerning the origin of the human body as coming from preexistent matter — for Catholic faith obliges us to hold that human souls are immediately created by God — be investigated and discussed by experts as far as the present state of human science and sacred theology allow" (no. 36). Pius also ruled out polygenism, which holds that after Adam there existed true humans not descended from him. Adam was an actual individual and not a name representing a number of first parents. Polygenism, Pius wrote, cannot be reconciled with the revealed truths about original sin (cf. no. 37).

Pius XII had a keen interest in modern science, and in this respect John Paul II is very much his intellectual successor. Throughout his papacy, John Paul has campaigned for a more fruitful dialogue between science and Catholic theology. Among his earliest acts as pope was to ask a commission of scholars to study the Galileo affair. Contrary to reports in the media, he was not on this occasion throwing in the towel and admitting that the earth goes around the sun. That particular issue, so far as the Church is concerned, had been settled as long ago as 1741 when Benedict XIV bid the Holy Office grant an imprimatur to the collected works of Galileo. What the pope wanted was for both scientists and theologians to have a clearer view of the affair, which helped precipitate the tragic split between faith and science in the seventeenth century from which Western culture has not recovered.

A Digression on Galileo

Since the Galileo episode inevitably arises in any discussion about the Catholic Church and science, the commission's report is worth a digression. The commission affirmed that Church authorities in the seventeenth century had gravely violated Galileo's rights as a scientist; but it also interestingly supported the anti-Catholic T. H. Huxley, who examined the Galileo case and reluctantly concluded that "the Church had the best of it." The great irony is that until Galileo forced the issue into the realm of theology, the Church had been a willing ombudsman for the new astronomy that emerged in the sixteenth century. In 1543, Nicolai Copernicus, a Polish canon and devout Catholic, published his epochal book supporting the heliocentric (earth around the sun) model at the urging of two Catholic prelates, dedicating it to Pope Paul III, who received it cordially.

If the issue had remained purely scientific, Church authorities would have shrugged it off. Galileo's mistake was to push the debate onto theological grounds; he told the Church: Either support the heliocentric model as fact (even though not proven) or condemn it. He refused the reasonable middle ground offered by Cardinal Bellarmine: You are welcome to hold the Copernican model as a hypothesis; you may even assert that it is superior to the old Ptolemaic model; but don't tell us to reinterpret Scripture until you have proof.

Galileo's response was his theory of the tides, which purported to show that the tides are caused by the earth's rotation. Even some of Galileo's supporters could see that this was nonsense. Also, ignoring the work of Kepler, he insisted that the planets go around the earth in perfect circles, which the Jesuit astronomers could plainly see was untenable. In fact, the Copernican system was not strictly "proved" until 1838, when Friedrich Bessel succeeded in determining the parallax of star 61 Cygni.

The real issue in the Galileo affair was the literal interpretation of Scripture. In 1616, the year of Galileo's first trial, there was precious little elasticity in Catholic biblical theology. But this was also the case among Protestants. Luther and Melanchthon had vehemently opposed the heliocentric model on scriptural grounds. Luther, in fact, had the privilege of being the first churchman to call Copernicus a "fool." Another irony of the affair was pointed out by John Paul II: Galileo's argument that Scripture often makes use of figurative language and is meant to teach "how to go to heaven, not how the heavens go," was eventually made in two great papal encyclicals, Leo XIII's *Providentissimus Deus* (1893) and Pius XII's *Divino Afflante Spiritu* (1943).

John Paul II and Evolution

Pope John Paul II broached the subject of evolution during a series of general audiences in 1986 (specifically January 24 and April 16), in which he stated the following about the first chapter of Genesis:

> This text has above all a religious and theological importance. There are not to be sought in it significant elements from the point of view of the natural sciences. Research on the origin and development of individual species in nature does not find in this description any definitive norm. . . . Indeed, the theory of natural evolution, understood in a sense that does not exclude divine causality, is not in principle opposed to the truth about the creation of the invisible world, as presented in the Book of Genesis. . . . It must, however, be added that this hypothesis proposes only a probability, not a scientific certainty. The doctrine of faith, however, invariably affirms that man's spiritual soul is created directly by God. According to the hypothesis mentioned, it is possible that the human body, following the order

impressed by the Creator on the energies of life, could
have been gradually prepared in the forms of antecedent living beings.

In the highly publicized 1996 letter to the Pontifical
Academy of Sciences, John Paul reaffirmed the "methodological conditions" laid down by Pius XII concerning the study of
evolution: The theory cannot be adopted as though it were a
"certain, proven doctrine, and as though one could totally
prescind from revelation with regard to the questions it
raises"; and, "theories of evolution which, in accordance with
the philosophies inspiring them, consider spirit as emerging
from forces of living matter or as mere epiphenomenon of
this matter, are incompatible with the truth about man. Nor
are they able to ground the dignity of the human person."

The pope's letter recognized the controversy among
evolutionists, stating that "rather than speaking about the
theory of evolution, it is more accurate to speak of theories
of evolution. The use of the plural is required here . . . because of the diversity of explanations regarding the theories
of evolution." The pope's most controversial (and mistrans-
lated) statement was his calling evolution "more than a hypothesis" (*"plus qu 'une hypothèse"* in the original French
text). The pope was not thereby saying that evolution is a
proven fact. Rather, in accord with general scientific termi-
nology, he was saying that we may regard evolution as a *theory*
— which is to say, a model of some explanatory value that is
nonetheless far from being satisfactorily verified by scientists. The pope actually exercised restraint in refraining from
commenting on the paucity of scientific evidence for any
macroevolutionary mechanism.

The pope flatly rejected evolutionary theories that are
philosophical materialism tricked up as science, which is what

we find in books by Darwinists. Scientists like Dawkins and Carl Sagan start with a philosophical premise: There is no God. This allows them to banish teleology, or purpose, from the discussion, making Darwin the only possible contender. In fact, the pope would have clarified matters greatly if he had repeated the observation of a number of Catholic philosophers that the real debate is not over evolution *per se*, but teleology. Either man is the accidental product of purely natural forces, or he is not.

But the position of the Magisterium regarding evolution is clear. It makes no difference whether man is descended biologically from some apelike creature, so long as we understand that there had to be what John Paul calls an "ontological leap" between that creature and the first human person. This would have involved the direct action of God, who creates each rational soul out of nothing. As a result, man is a being profoundly different from the rest of the animal kingdom, no matter what his biological antecedents. Man is a *person* made in the image of God. Dogs and chimps are not. This truth is taught by Genesis. But the Church is warning us that the Sacred Author does not in addition mean to give scientific information about how God's creation of man unfolded in the natural order, whether it was done in a flash or over many eons.

How to Read the Book of Genesis

The confusion over evolution among Christians boils down to the question of how to read the creation account in Genesis. In his letter, John Paul simply reiterated what the Magisterium has argued tirelessly since Leo XIII's *Providentissimus Deus.* Scripture does not teach science, period. Unfortunately there are still biblical fundamentalists, Catholic and Protestant, who do not grasp this simple point.

When Christ said that the mustard seed was the smallest of seeds (and it is about the size of a speck of dust) he was not laying down a principle of botany. In fact, botanists tell us there are smaller seeds. Our Lord was simply talking to the men of his time in their own language, and with reference to their own experience. Hence, the warning of Pius XII in *Divino Afflante Spiritu* that the true sense of a biblical passage is not always obvious, as the authors of Sacred Scripture wrote in the idioms of their time and place.

As Catholics, we must believe that every word of Scripture is inspired by the Holy Spirit (a claim the Church will not make even for the Magisterium's *ex cathedra* pronouncements); but we must not think of its authors as going into a trance and taking automatic dictation in a "pure" language untouched by historical contingency. Rather, God made full use of the writers' habits of mind and expression. It's the old mystery of grace and free will.

Genesis was written in the archaic, prescientific idiom of the ancient Palestinians. Its author could not have told us that the universe is twelve billion years old because the Hebrews did not have a word for one billion and the information is not necessary for our salvation. The Hebrew word for day — *yom* — can mean a twenty-four-hour day, or a longer period. If the universe were roughly six thousand years old, as a literal reading of Genesis would suggest, then we would not be able to see the Milky Way. The light would not have reached the earth yet.

A modern reader of Genesis must bear in mind the principles of biblical exegesis laid down by St. Augustine in his great work *De Genesi ad Litteram*, mentioned earlier. Augustine taught that whenever reason established with certainty a fact about the physical world, seemingly contrary statements in the Bible must be interpreted accordingly. He opposed the idea of a "Christian account" of natural phenomena in opposition to what could be known by science. He viewed such accounts as "most deplorable and harmful, and to be avoided at any cost," because on hearing them the non-believer "could hardly hold his laughter on seeing, as the saying goes, the error raise sky-high."

As early as the year 410, then, the greatest of the Western Church Fathers was telling us that the Book of Genesis is not a textbook in astrophysics or geology. Augustine himself was a kind of evolutionist, speculating that God's creation of the cosmos was an instantaneous act whose effects unfolded over a long period. God had planted "rational seeds" in nature that eventually fructified into the diversity of plants and animals we see today. St. Thomas Aquinas cites this view of Augustine's more than once in the *Summa Theologiae*.

St. Thomas, Gilson writes, "was well aware that the Book of Genesis was not a treatise on cosmography for the use of scholars. It was a statement of the truth intended for the simple people whom Moses was addressing. Thus it is sometimes possible to interpret it in a variety of ways. So it was that when we speak of the six days of creation, we can understand by it either six successive days, as do Ambrose, Basil, Chrysostom and Gregory, and is suggested by the letter of the text. . . . Or we can with Augustine take it to refer to the simultaneous creation of all beings with days symbolizing the various orders of beings. This second interpretation is at first sight less literal, but is, rationally speaking, more satisfying. It is the one that St. Thomas adopts, although he does not exclude the other which, as he says, can also be held."

Seven hundred years later, Cardinal Augustin Bea, the German Jesuit biblical scholar who helped Pius XII draft *Divino Afflante Spiritu*, wrote that the first Book of Genesis does not deal with the "true constitution of things visible."

It is meant to convey truths outside the scientific order.

While they do not teach science, the early chapters of Genesis *are* history and not myth. But they are not history as it would be written by a modern historian. (It is not as though there was a camcorder in the Garden of Eden.) You might say that they are history written in mythic language — a poetic compression of the truth, as it were. We are obliged to believe the fundamental truths expressed by the Sacred Author — for example, that our first parents, tempted by the devil, committed a primal act of disobedience whose effects we still suffer. But the Catholic doctrine of original sin is entirely outside the realm of science. It's worth keeping in mind, however, Newman's remark that the more he contemplated humanity, the clearer it became to him that the race was "implicated in some terrible aboriginal calamity."

The Literalist Temptation

Biblical fundamentalism — and its corollary, creation science — is a distinctly Protestant phenomenon. Although it has roots in the commentaries on Genesis written by Luther and Calvin, its real beginning was in nineteenth-century America. Biblical literalism was erected as a defense against the onslaught of rationalist criticism launched by German scholars intent on undermining Christian belief in the inerrancy of Scripture. Protestant evangelicals, whose religion was highly fideist to begin with, took refuge in a semantic literalism that sheltered the Bible from the invasive procedures of agnostic scholarship. The intellectual simplicity and doctrinal clarity of this position make it attractive to some Catholics today. This appeal is understandable. They are seeking refuge from the predations of heterodox theologians, who seem as eager as their nineteenth-century forebears to deconstruct the faith.

The temptation to biblical literalism should be resisted, however. The Bible was never meant to be read apart from the teaching authority of the Church established by Christ. Although the fact is understandably overlooked by our Protestant friends, it was not until the end of the fourth century that the twenty-seven books that comprise the New Testament were agreed upon by two ecumenical councils, subject to final approval by the pope. And it was the Church that insisted, against the protests of heretics, that the Old Testament be included in the Christian canon. The Bible was never meant to stand alone as a separate authority. It is the Church, the Mystical Body of Christ, that preserves the deposit of the faith, of which Scripture is a part. St. Augustine, as usual, got it exactly right: "But for the authority of the Catholic Church, I would not believe the Gospel."

Since Leo XIII, the Magisterium has progressively discouraged the literalist reading of Genesis favored by Protestants. Can a Catholic nonetheless read Genesis as a literal scientific treatise? Yes, if he wants to — but he will not be reading Scripture with the mind of the Church. He will find himself in the dilemma of trying to force scientific data into a biblical template that was never meant to receive it. And he will be severely handicapped in doing apologetics in a post-Christian world. He will, in fact, be the reverse of apostolic if he tries to explain to anyone the doctrine of creation in terms of ancient Hebrew cosmology.

The test of a first-rate intellect, it has been said, is the ability to hold two seemingly opposed ideas and retain the ability to function. The creation account in Genesis is true, but it is not scientifically "true." A brilliant twentieth-century Catholic apologist, Frank J. Sheed, wrote of the creation account in his masterpiece, *Theology and Sanity*. His words are an invitation to Catholics tempted by biblical literalism to use their reason and not take refuge in overly simplistic readings of Scripture. The author of Genesis, Sheed writes, "tells us of the fact but not the process: there was an assembly of elements of the material universe, but was it instantaneous or spread over a considerable space and time? Was it complete in one act, or by stages? Were those elements, for instance, formed into an animal body that as one generation followed another gradually evolved — not, of course, by the ordinary laws of matter but under the special guidance of God — to a point where it was capable of union with a spiritual soul, which God created and infused into it? The statement in Genesis does not seem actually to exclude this, but it certainly does not say it. Nor has the Church formally said that it is not so. . . ."

If asked his views about Darwin, an intelligent Catholic might say something like this: "The hypothesis of the common biological descent of species is interesting and worth exploring. But a hypothesis is one thing, and proofs and demonstrations are another. Common descent (oh, all right — call it 'evolution,' although the fossils suggest a phrase like 'abrupt appearance') is no more than an inference based on similarities of body plans and the fact that all creatures are genetically coded. But a purely *naturalistic* theory of evolution like Darwin's is going to have trouble explaining the discontinuities between major animal groups and the sudden appearance of new species. Nobody, in fact, has ever seen one species change into another. Macroevolution, Darwinian or otherwise, is a theory in search of a real event. The claim that natural selection explains all biological phenomena is supported neither by empirical evidence nor logical argument. Darwin can explain why there are different breeds of dog; he cannot explain the origin of the higher animal groups. Nor are we any closer than the Victorians to explaining the origin of life. Life only seems to come from life. But even if some day the origin of life were proven to be a mechanistic phenomenon (which is not very likely), I would be unperturbed, because such a mechanism would not be incompatible with the Catholic doctrine of creation. Creation from nothing is beyond scientific explanation. The greatest scientific genius will never be able to produce *being*, or even to discuss it with his scientific vocabulary. Ditto for human consciousness."

Finally, the Church insists that humankind is not an accident; that no matter how he went about creating *Homo sapiens*, God from all eternity intended man and all creation to exist in their present form. Catholics are not obliged to square scientific data with the early verses of Genesis, whose truths — and they are truths, not myth — are expressed in words addressed to an early people whose understanding of the physical world was very different from our own. And, as Pope John Paul II keeps insisting, Catholics can anticipate with serenity modern scientific discoveries that, more often than not, raise fundamental questions science itself cannot answer.

Chapter Nine

The *Origin of Species* Revisited: Modern Christian Writers and Darwin

"There is no worse metaphysics than disguised metaphysics." — Jacques Maritain

A Reasonable Catholic Center

Since the theory of evolution, in the words of John Paul II, is "an essential subject which deeply interests the Church," it is inevitable that major Catholic thinkers address the issue. Each of the writers below deals with the subject in his own inimitable way. Chesterton the journalist relies on brilliant flashes of intuition. Belloc is combative and makes effective use of his French reading. Maritain and Gilson put the issue in a Thomistic framework. All, including the Anglican C. S. Lewis, take a "realist" approach to science and locate a reasonable Catholic center between the philosophical materialism of Darwinists and the biblical literalism of fundamentalists. Their commonsense criticisms of Darwin's theory have held up well in light of later scientific research.

The Catholic thinker most identified with evolution, the French Jesuit paleontologist Pierre Teilhard de Chardin, can be dealt with in a few sentences. He does not loom as large on the Catholic intellectual landscape as he did a generation ago.

Teilhard concocted from evolutionary theory a kind of process theology that, among other things, implicitly denies the doctrine of original sin. Pope Pius XII once asked the great French theologian Étienne Gilson to write a critique of Teilhard's work. Gilson replied that such a task was impossible because Teilhard's books were poetry and not philosophy. You cannot "refute" a poem. Even Teilhard's serious defenders, like Henri de Lubac, make constant apologies for his imprecise use of language. But habitual imprecision with words is a kind of primal offense in a theologian. Teilhard is one of those seductive thinkers, like Montaigne, who bristle with arresting insights and turns of phrase. But if you search their writings for a coherent metaphysics, you find yourself pursuing a vapor. "You cannot get any benefit or any enlightenment from thinking about Teilhard," Gilson wrote to de Lubac. "The ravages he wrought, which I have witnessed, are horrifying."

St. George Jackson Mivart (1827-1900)

Mivart, the talented English biologist, was the son of the owner of Claridges, the most famous hotel in London. To the distress of his parents, he converted to Catholicism at the age of sixteen. Thus excluded from the universities, he studied law at Lincoln's Inn, which may account for the forensic brilliance of his critique of Darwin. Instead of entering the legal profession, however, he took up biology, befriending the biggest names in the field, people like Darwin, Huxley, and Owen.

At first Mivart was noncommittal about the *Origin of Species*. But gradually he changed his mind: "It was in 1868 that difficulties as to the theory of Natural Selection began to take shape in my mind. . . . After many painful days . . . I felt it my duty first of all to go straight to Professor Huxley and tell him all my thoughts . . . including the theological aspect of the question. Never before or since have I had a more painful experience than fell to my lot in his room at the School of Mines on that 15th of June, 1869. As soon as I had made my meaning clear, his countenance became transformed as I had never seen it. Yet he looked more sad and surprised than anything else. He was kind and gentle as he said regretfully, but most firmly, that nothing so united or severed men as questions such as those I had spoken of."

In 1871, Mivart published *On the Genesis of Species*. The book was the most compelling attack on the theory of natural selection to be published in Darwin's lifetime. Superbly written and argued, the book is still cited in the professional literature of biology. (Stephen Jay Gould, who entertains similar doubts about the explanatory power of natural selection, occasionally refers to Mivart.) Mivart accepted the hypothesis of evolution, or common descent; but he thought the *Origin* an intellectual muddle. Darwin had not adequately answered the obvious objections to his theory. With great force and clarity, Mivart argued that natural selection was unable to explain "the incipient, infinitesimal beginnings of structures which are of utility only when they are considerably developed."

This point against Darwin's theory has never been satisfactorily refuted. And Mivart rightly dismissed Darwin's strategy for dealing with it: "It is no reply to this to say, what is no doubt abstractly true, that whatever is possible becomes probable, if only time enough be allowed. There are improbabilities so great that the common sense of mankind treats them as impossibilities. It is not, for instance, in the strictest sense of the word, impossible that a poem and a mathematical proposition should be obtained by the process of shaking letters out of a box; but it is improbable to a degree that cannot be distinguished from impossibility; and the improbability of obtaining an improvement in an organ by means of several spontaneous generations, all occurring together, is an improbability of the same kind."

How did Mivart explain evolution? First, he argued that "evolution" and the Christian idea of "creation" are not antagonistic. "Creation is not a miraculous interference with the laws of nature, but the very institution of those laws." These laws, according to Mivart, must include an "internal innate force. . . . By such a force, from time to time, new species are manifested by ordinary generation. . . . These 'jumps' are considerable in comparison with the minute variations of 'Natural Selection.'. . ." The "latent tendency which exists to these sudden evolutions" is triggered "by the stimulus of external conditions." Mivart, then, was proposing a pattern of quantum jumps and demoting natural selection to a preservative rather than creative agent.

Mivart's vague mechanism — the "internal innate force" — is no more than a guess based on negative evidence. And Mivart's critics can be forgiven for pointing out that this "force" sounds metaphysical, even though Mivart insisted that it wasn't. Mivart seems to have been groping for the sort of solution favored by those modern biologists who, in the words of Ho and Saunders, think that the mechanism of macroevolution must be found in "the epigenetic processes involved in ontogeny itself." Translation: They are looking for internal "preprogrammed" genetic mechanisms that may cause "superfluous" DNA to suddenly organize itself into new forms. According to this theory, species do not evolve slowly into other species, but rather harbor the seeds of new species that appear quite suddenly. These sudden "saltational" jumps are anathema to Darwinists, because they seem miraculous and demote natural selection to a minor role. But Mivart expressly excluded miraculous interventions. His only supernatural agency is the initial divine fillip at the moment of creation. The rest is pure mechanism.

The *Genesis of Species* had a great effect on the public, swelling the reaction that was building against the theory of natural selection. Darwin called himself a "master wriggler" and on no occasion did he "wriggle" more than in his response to Mivart's criticisms. Darwin did not effectively answer Mivart's argument that natural selection is incapable of dealing with incipient structures, choosing to dwell instead on subordinate issues. Huxley wrote a savage review of the book, adopting the strategy (still used by Darwinists) of attacking Mivart's religion rather than answering his scientific objections. Mivart's reaction to Huxley's offensive deserves to be quoted: "It was not however without surprise that I learned that my one unpardonable sin — the one great offence disqualifying me from being 'a loyal soldier of science' — was my attempt to show that there is no real antagonism between the Christian revelation and evolution."

The Darwinian camp's subsequent treatment of Mivart was petty and vindictive. Although the tone of Mivart's criticism had been civil, Darwin and Huxley agreed that he had not "acted as a gentleman." They broke off relations with him, even though Mivart went to great lengths to remain on good terms. On several occasions they made sure that he was blackballed for membership in the prestigious Athenaeum Club, which Mivart wished to join. Like their successors today, they were relentless in excommunicating from the scientific establishment a person who had pointed out the logical fallacies of their position.

G. K. Chesterton (1874-1936)

Chesterton visited the issue of evolution repeatedly in his writings. His most sustained treatment of the subject is to be found in his masterpiece, *The Everlasting Man* (1925). That book was the product of two events: Chesterton's own conversion to Catholicism a few years earlier, and the phenomenal success of H. G. Wells's *Outline of History*, which was published in 1920 and revised in 1925. Wells was an enormously energetic and fluent writer; but his "modernity" amounted to little more than repackaging the stale intellectual remains of the nineteenth century. The loose evolutionism of the *Outline* irked Chesterton and Belloc, who both went on the offensive.

With his usual epigrammatic brilliance, Chesterton wrote that the idea of evolution was a kind of fogging agent used by materialists to hide ultimate metaphysical questions: "There is something slow and soothing and gradual about the word and even the idea. As a matter of fact, it is not, touching the primary things, a very practical word or a very profitable idea. Nobody can imagine how nothing could turn into something. Nobody can get an inch nearer to it by explaining how something could turn into something else."

Darwinian evolution, Chesterton argued, cannot tell us why there is a universe. Anybody who really understands this question, Chesterton writes, "will know that it always has been and always will be a religious question; or at any rate a philosophical or metaphysical question." No philosopher, moreover, can deny that "a mystery still attaches to the two great transitions: the origin of the universe itself and the origin of the principle of life itself. Most philosophers have the enlightenment to add that a third mystery attaches to the origin of man himself. In other words, a third bridge was built across a third abyss of the unthinkable when there came into the world what we call reason and what we call will." Man, according to Chesterton, is "not merely an evolution but rather a revolution."

Darwinists are never more awkward than when dealing with the three great "transitions" mentioned by Chesterton. When they address them at all, they tend to lapse into bad metaphysics. Thus, Theodosius Dobzhansky, one of the architects of neo-Darwinism, wrote that the origin of life and of man constituted two great "transcendences" in evolutionary history. This sounds suspiciously like slipping a metaphysical agent in the back door when natural selection doesn't seem up to the job. Similarly, Daniel Dennett, a leading spokesman for "ultra-Darwinism," tells us that the universe began with "next to nothing," an ontological category that Chesterton would have thought amusing. Either the universe began with something, or it began with nothing. Neither alternative is comforting to an atheist like Dennett. "Next to nothing" is simply verbal camouflage for his own metaphysical uneasiness about the massive facticity of creation.

Chesterton did not have a theological problem with the idea of evolution, pointing out: "If evolution simply means that a positive thing called an ape turned very slowly into a positive thing called a man, it is stingless for the most orthodox; for a personal God might just as well do things slowly as quickly, especially if, like the Christian God, he were outside time." Chesterton was no spokesman for creationism, Catholic or Protestant. He noted about Christian fundamentalists that "the funniest thing about them is their name. For whatever else the Fundamentalist is, he is not fundamental. He is content with the bare letter of Scripture — the translation of a translation — without venturing to ask for its original authority."

Chesterton also had no patience with Darwinism. He considered the theory of natural selection to be "an extravagantly improbable conjecture." And he was quick to catch its tautological structure: "Nature selecting those that vary in the most successful direction means nothing whatever except that the successful succeed." Chesterton thought the whole theory an offense against logic: "I am very far indeed from calling the Darwinian a liar; but I shall continue to say that he is not always a logician." He was also aware that sixty years of digging by paleontologists eager to prove Darwin right had not produced the required transitional forms: "If the proofs of natural selection are lost, why then, there are no proofs of natural selection; and there is an end of it."

But it was not Darwin's illogical arguments that really bothered Chesterton. It was his metaphysics. The theory destroyed all forms and contours, turning everything into a chaotic flux. Darwinists, he wrote, see everything in "gray gradations of twilight" because "they believe it is the twilight of the gods." Chesterton, Jaki remarks, abhorred evolutionary materialism, because "it abolishes forms and all that goes with them, including that deepest kind of ontological form which is the immortal human soul." Man did not so much mind seeing his distant reflection in the local zoo. "All normal men could for a practical joke make beasts of themselves as well as their grandfathers." Rather, their dismay was at the realization that "when once one begins to think of man as a shifting and alterable thing, it is always easy for the strong and crafty to twist him into new shapes for all kinds of unnatural purposes."

Chesterton's objection to Darwinism, then, was anthropological: "Evolution does not specially deny the existence of God; what it does deny is the existence of man." And for Chesterton, the existence of man could not be discussed apart from the dogma of the Incarnation. Christ had an immortal human soul. Darwinists insist that there is no such thing. This is the fundamental point where Catholic orthodoxy and philosophical Darwinism can never be reconciled. Chesterton would have been pained by Catholic academics who uncritically accept Darwin's anthropology so as not to offend the secular orthodoxies that reign unchallenged in many Catholic institutions.

Hilaire Belloc (1870-1953)

Hilaire Belloc, like Chesterton, did not like Darwinism partly because it was so obviously a product of the ethos of industrial capitalism. And he shared Chesterton's low regard for Wells's *Outline of History*. The most combative of Catholic apologists, Belloc mounted an aggressive campaign against the book. His ferocity was no doubt provoked by Wells's constant harangues against Catholicism. Wells, who had been raised by a mother who was bitterly anti-Catholic, never missed an opportunity to attack the Church. His ravings against Catholicism reached a crescendo in 1943, when he published a pamphlet, *Crux Ansata: An Indictment of the Catholic Church*, which, in effect, urged the Allies to bomb Rome because the pope was there. Belloc may also have been motivated by commercial jealousy. He had written one historical potboiler after another (mostly biographies that are very good of their kind) with nothing like the financial success of the *Outline of History*.

Month after month, Belloc wrote scathing essays about Wells's book in the Catholic magazine *The Universe*. These were collected in *A Companion to H. G. Wells's Outline of History*. The second chapter, "Mr. Wells and the Creation of the World," is one of the best critiques of Darwin's theory ever written.

Belloc did not have a religious problem with evolution. He was not a biblical literalist, although he went a bit far in complaining that the Catholic Church was saddled with the "Hebrew folklore" of Genesis. "Evolution in general is not the point," Belloc wrote. "It involves no fundamental issue. It clashes with no theology or philosophy. . . . It is when men come to discuss *how* the difference between varying types arose that we enter upon a quarrel between opposing philosophies, Christian and anti-Christian." And he added: "It is obvious that if the system of blind chance were demonstrably true, those great modern intellects who say in their hearts, 'There is no God,' have a powerful weapon in the theory of Natural Selection. They seized upon that weapon with gusto; and they are still desperately clinging to the handle though the business part of the instrument has long been battered shapeless. . . ."

Belloc systematically dismantled the philosophical and scientific pretensions of Darwinism. He relied heavily on prominent French biologists — Cuenot, Delage, Vialleton — and here he had an advantage over Wells, whose French was not very good. Wells, notoriously thin-skinned, was not temperamentally suited to engage in the sort of polemical mudslinging in which Belloc delighted. Friends like the novelist Arnold Bennett warned Wells not to tangle with Belloc. Chesterton gave the careful advice that "Hilary is not an enemy whom I would choose. . . ."

Wells, nonetheless, published *Mr. Belloc Objects to the Outline of History* in 1926, to which his adversary quickly responded with *Mr. Belloc Still Objects.* Finally, Wells challenged Belloc to find a factual error in the *Outline,* and this was his fatal mistake. Belloc's response was to quote page 55 of the book, where Wells wrote that Paleolithic man "did not know of the bow. . . ." Belloc remarked that he was stunned that "a person pretending to teach popular prehistorical science in 1925 should tell us of the cave painters that it was 'doubtful they knew of the bow' . . . because here before me, in Mr. Wells's own book, are reproductions of these cave paintings, with the bow and arrow appearing all over them."

Wells finally begged off, and Belloc claimed victory. In his memoirs, Malcolm Muggeridge called Wells the "comic ombudsman of the modern age." This was in reference to Wells's trying to persuade Stalin to join the PEN Club, but the description nicely fits Wells as a popular spokesman for Darwin. (PEN is an acronym for "poets, playwrights, editors, essayists, and novelists.")

Jacques Maritain (1882-1973)

Jacques Maritain, Catholic convert and great French Thomist, was highly conversant with modern science. He not only read an enormous quantity of scientific literature but also studied and corresponded with great scientific figures like Driesch and Einstein. The data of modern science, in his view, merely confirmed the Thomistic understanding of the cosmos. The work of biologists and astronomers had no more ardent supporter. And yet, it was Maritain who coined the word "scientism" to described what he called a "false intellectual currency" put into circulation by scientists when they stepped outside their proper sphere and began to philosophize. Maritain was a champion of the Thomistic hierarchy of knowledge, and he insisted that the data of science had to be properly mediated by a philosophy of nature, which in turn is nourished by metaphysics, which is the philosophical penetration of being itself.

Although he was a giant of twentieth-century philosophy and (according to Pope Paul VI) a seminal influence on the Second Vatican Council, Maritain's stock among Catholic thinkers was already in sharp decline at the time of his death. Deal Hudson has argued that the cause of this seemingly inexplicable neglect was the scathing critique of Teilhard de Chardin in one of Maritain's last books, *The Peasant of the Garonne* (1967). Teilhard was an icon of post-Vatican II liberal theology, and Maritain's dismissal of his philosophy as "one more Christian gnosis . . . like all gnoses — a bad gnosis" did not sit well with what Maritain referred to as Teilhard's "enraptured ecclesiastical retinue."

What Maritain objected to was Teilhard's "purely *evolutive conception* where being is replaced by becoming and every essence . . . vanishes." Maritain had no objection to the theory of evolution *per se*. In fact, he thought that a long history of transmutations leading up to man was compatible with Thomistic philosophy. While St. Thomas himself "had no idea of what we call Evolution," he had nonetheless given us the "true basis of a philosophy of Evolution." All that was necessary was to extend through the vast reaches of geological time the Thomistic hierarchy of degrees of perfection.

Maritain's thoughts on evolution are mostly contained in a conference, "Toward a Thomistic Idea of Evolution," given in Toulouse in 1967. It was meant to be the first of four. Unfortunately, Maritain did not have the strength to complete the series, and his ideas on the subject are in the nature of a preliminary sketch. The conference is nonetheless a *tour de force* of applied Thomism that deserves serious attention.

There is, according to St. Thomas, a metaphysical tendency or aspiration in all matter toward higher and higher forms. Each being in nature tends not only toward its own good but also toward a higher level of perfection. Starting with prime matter, each degree of being is "in potency" toward the next higher stage of being. And so we have an upward striving of prime matter toward the basic elements; of the elements toward compounds; and of compounds toward the "vegetable soul" that is the substantial form of the plant.

The vegetative soul, St. Thomas continues (in the *Summa Contra Gentiles*), "is in potency to the sensitive soul [the form of animals], as the sensitive soul is to the intellective soul [the form of man]. . . . Indeed man is the end of the whole movement of generation."

For Maritain, evolution is this dynamic of "potency" and "act" played out over millennia until its culmination in man. The history of life shows the "transnatural ontological tendency or aspiration" of all beings to "become — at least in their descendants — better than they are." Two different causalities are involved: first, the causality of the Creator of being; and then the secondary causality of living beings themselves, "whose immanent activity, under the superelevating motion of the first Cause . . . discovers something new." Maritain's version of evolution, which he admitted to be speculative and not subject to scientific verification, would involve quantum leaps between species as the form or soul of each was replaced by the next higher. Only in passing does Maritain refer to the "pitiful extrinsic mechanism" of Darwinian selection as being of no account in this process.

Man, according to Maritain, may have been preceded by overdeveloped animals whom he calls "hominians." These represented the highest kind of organism that could be perfected by the sensitive (or animal) soul. Although without intellect, they were "already groping in the vicinity of the spirit" and were "undoubtedly less well equipped . . . with that innate knowledge which is part of the instincts of animals without reason, and consequently were less fitted to defend themselves against their enemies." These "hominians" were the immediate ancestors of man, but only in potency. At some point, God "by an absolutely free act" chose a particular hominian couple, with the purpose of infusing in them "in the course of the prenatal life of these living beings" an intellective and immortal soul, "which will have been called for by an ultimate disposition of matter, produced in the hominian fetus or fetuses . . . and this soul will in a very particular way already be human."

The prehuman couple or couples, Maritain writes, "are not the father and mother of the human race . . . because it is from God, and created by Him, that man receives the soul which makes him a man. . . ." As St. Luke says in tracing Jesus' lineage, we are descended from Seth, who was the son of Adam, who was the son of God. Maritain's scheme fully preserves the "ontological leap" between man and other animals that Pope John Paul II says is fundamental to any Christian anthropology.

Maritain closes with a brief look at polygenism, which, *contra* Rahner and other theologians, he insists must be rejected. If we look at God's way of doing things, Maritain writes, "it seems to us that each time a historical change of immense importance took place, God wills that it be the work of one person alone (or of two alone)." This was the case with Abraham, Moses, John the Baptist, the Virgin Mary, St. Paul — and (Maritain can't resist adding) Albert the Great and St. Thomas. So, he concludes, "What is so astonishing about the fact that Revelation should teach us that the human nature of each of us has its origin in a single human couple. . . ?"

Étienne Gilson (1884-1978)

Étienne Gilson, the French Thomist philosopher and historian, did not stop writing until shortly before his death at age ninety-four in 1978. His critique of Darwin's theory, *From Aristotle to Darwin and Back Again* (1971), is an extraordinary performance for an octogenarian. Gilson not only displays an encyclopedic knowledge of writers like Lamarck, Darwin, and Spencer but also analyzes the philosophical issues with implacable lucidity. As a historian of ideas, he is struck at how the intellectual maneuvers of neo-Darwinism resemble those of Scholastic philosophy in its late, decadent phase in the fourteenth century. And as a Frenchman, he is amused by the American tendency to take evolutionary Darwinism for a phenomenon "of planetary significance."

Any discussion of evolution, Gilson writes, must be preceded by a careful examination of the underlying philosophical issues. No matter what one's position on Darwin, one cannot write on the subject without, consciously or unconsciously, making philosophical statements. Darwin himself, according to Gilson, often strayed beyond science and into the realm of philosophy. Whenever he did so, he got into trouble. Darwin is a master observer of nature; but in trying to turn his observations into a theory, "he displays an intellectual nonchalance and an imprecision in ideas which does not appear in any way tolerable."

Darwin's philosophical problems begin with his use of the words "origin" and "species": "From the very beginning a serious imprecision was introduced into the definition of the very object of the book, for at no time did Darwin undertake to clarify the issue of the origin of species, in the sense of the origin of the existence of species. He did not ask himself how it came about that there were species, but rather, given their existence, how it came about that they were such as they were. The problem of the absolute origin of species will never be posed by Darwin."

A more accurate title for Darwin's book, according to Gilson, would be the *Origin of Varieties*. Darwin's use of the word "species," moreover, is contradictory. "To say that species are fixed," Gilson writes, "is a tautology; to say that they change is to say that they do not exist. Why does Darwin so obstinately say that they transform themselves, rather than saying simply that they do not exist?"

There are three metaphysical concepts that an evolutionist cannot avoid addressing: mechanism, final causality, and teleology. The great merit of Gilson's book is that it explains these ideas and how they tend to be misused by modern scientists eager to philosophize about their data. His discussion profitably starts with Aristotle. To the question "How does nature produce beings of such marvelous and intricate design?" Aristotle responds with another question: "How does man fabricate art?" Just as a work of art has its ultimate, or final, cause in the initial idea in the mind of the artist — one that cannot be measured by science — so the far more ingenious designs in nature must have an immaterial "final cause" outside of themselves.

"The analogy of art," Gilson writes, "assists us to recognize the presence in nature of a cause analogous to that which is intelligence in the operations of man, but we do not know what this cause is. The notion of a teleology without consciousness and immanent in nature remains mysterious to us. Aristotle does not think that this should be a reason to deny its existence."

Teleology comes from the Greek word *telos*, or end. The teleology of an organism is not a "thing" that can be observed by science, but exists nonetheless. The *telos* of an arrow speeding toward a target cannot be separated from the arrow and examined by science; nonetheless, there was an archer who aimed and shot the arrow. "The biologist is in a similar situation: he observes, to the exclusion of all teleology, something which could not exist without that teleology. . . ." But if the biologist goes on to assert that there is no "final cause" of his subject, then he is in the position of dealing with a speeding arrow while insisting that there is no archer who shot it. Even the most obdurate materialist has difficulty, when speaking of the function of an organ or of a tissue, not brushing against the idea of teleology.

The debate between mechanism (which argues that there is nothing beyond the immediate push-and-pull of natural phenomena) and teleology (which argues that there is) involves a confusion of realms that ought to be kept separate. Gilson writes that Aristotle "never denied that the mechanism of Empedocles was true, but he reproached him with presenting it as a total explanation of reality in the order of living beings. . . ." Mechanistic explanations of reality, which are the legitimate business of science, can tell us much about how structures operate, but they cannot explain the existence of those structures. On this question, the biologist must yield the floor to philosophy.

But, Gilson continues, "If we ask the philosopher, What is teleology? It is his turn to be embarrassed." The difficulty is trying to define teleology "as if it were, in the living being, something distinct from that being." Here we arrive at a difficult metaphysical point, where we again encounter our archer: "The causes immanent in the being do not have any other real being than its own. Matter, form, and the end are real constituents of being, but they only exist in it and by it. . . . Whatever may be the transcendent origin of it, the teleology of the organism is in it as, once let fly by the archer, that of the arrow which flies to the target without knowing it, is in the arrow."

Organisms, then, have an immaterial element that cannot be isolated for scientific investigation. Where did this immaterial element come from? Aristotle's reply was: "From without." Like the human soul, we know it only by its effects. And its existence is in no way disproved by the fact that it cannot be measured by an instrument.

Gilson did not need the Second Vatican Council to remind him that science ought to be allowed its proper methodology. Indeed, for Gilson, science "cannot be too positivistic." He was full of admiration for the scientific fecundity of the mechanist approach to nature. But when that mechanism is used to explain all of nature — in other words, to "resolve the philosophical problem to which finalism is the response" — it becomes an absurdity. The only explanation at its disposal is "chance." Yet chance, according to Gilson, is not an explanation, but the absence of one. To say that the intricate design of the eye is due to accident is to say precisely nothing.

Natural selection, which is the accumulation of accidents, cannot therefore qualify as an explanation of anything. Gilson finds nothing but philosophical comedy in the statements of Darwinists that natural selection generates improbable wonders, since "scientifically, as well as philosophically, the mechanism of natural selection is simply a nonexplanation." Of Darwin's "one long argument" in the *Origin*, Gilson, who throughout gives the impression of treating a sophomoric thinker with tact and cordiality, writes: "One does not know how to demonstrate that [the immense accumulation of sheer chances] is *impossible*, but one can at least observe that the affirmation of it is totally arbitrary and is only justified by the previous refusal of all other forms of explanation."

Gilson closes with words that ought to be affixed like a warning label to books like Dawkins's *The Blind Watchmaker*: "Instead of trying to make us take as scientific truths the long train of reveries over which their imagination dallies, scientists would render us the greatest service by warning us as precisely as possible, each time, of the point where their thought, impatient of the rigors of proof, grants itself the pleasure of intelligently imagining what it no longer hopes to know."

C. S. Lewis (1898-1963)

C. S. Lewis was the greatest English-speaking Christian apologist of the twentieth century. Although acutely aware of the moral and intellectual corruptions of Darwinism, he addressed the issue only in passing. One of his biographers, A. N. Wilson, tells us that when, on one occasion, someone sitting at table in the Lewis household made a silly materialist remark, Lewis blurted out: "Oh, we have a Darwinist at the table!" His most sustained comments on the ideology of "evolutionism" are in the essay "The Funeral of a Great Myth," where he writes that he has heard of this myth called "Wellsianity," but he will refer to it as evolutionism.

In this myth, evolution is the "formula for all existence . . . even though scientists cannot explain the origin of life or of the universe." Like Chesterton, Lewis thought that the evolutionists' glib treatment of major ontological issues amounted to a species of intellectual fraud. He made three telling points about evolutionism:

> • He quotes in that essay a biologist named D.M.S. Watson, who admitted that Darwin's theory "is accepted by zoologists not because it has been observed to occur or . . . can be proved by logically coherent evidence to be true, but because the only alternative, special creation, is clearly incredible."
>
> • In his book *Miracles*, Lewis brilliantly exposes the fatal flaw of all modernist ideologies. Darwin, Marx, and Freud all said in one way or another that the human mind is the product of blind, irrational forces. But you cannot have it both ways — that humans are es-

sentially irrational, but that my rational arguments for evolutionary materialism are true.

    • Scientific methodology has been so successful in its own sphere that modern man has come to the conclusion that nothing that cannot be explained by science has any validity. This scientistic attitude lies at the root of modernity's "abolition of man."

Lewis's published correspondence shows that he was divided about going public with his objections to Darwinism. Around 1950, the Evolution Protest Movement, which had been founded by the ornithologist Douglas Dewar and the journalist Bernard Acworth, approached Lewis for a public endorsement. But Lewis, believing like Chesterton and Belloc that evolution in itself did not contradict Christian doctrine, refused to take sides or even write a preface to one of their books. He feared that his siding with the anti-Darwinists would damage his credibility as an apologist. He wrote to Acworth: "When a man has become a popular apologist, he must watch his step. Everyone is on the look-out for things that might discredit him."

Privately, however, Lewis found the group's scientific arguments against neo-Darwinism compelling — and the philosophical pretensions of Darwinian biologists repellent. He wrote to Acworth in 1951: "I wish I were younger. What inclines me now to think that you may be right in regarding [Darwinism] as *the* central and radical lie in the whole web of falsehood that now governs our lives is not so much your arguments against it as the fanatical and twisted attitudes of its defenders."

Chapter Ten

"In the Beginning . . .": The Mystery of Creation

Putting God Back in the Picture

In 1878, Newman's Anglican friend and fellow tractarian E. B. Pusey preached a sermon entitled "Un-Science, Not Science, Adverse to the Faith." The title might stand as a motto for anyone approaching the faith-versus-science debate. The Church has nothing to fear from science, but it has to be on guard against false philosophies pretending to be science. One of the valuable services of certain Christian thinkers has been to keep us alert to the fact that philosophical materialism often precedes, rather than follows, scientific thinking. Scratch a physicist like Stephen Hawking or a biologist like Ernst Mayr, and you will find a person who won't do science without first putting on philosophical blinders.

Pusey had no trouble demonstrating that the philosophy behind Darwin's scientific thinking was incoherent. He also made it clear that he had no objection to what he called "transformist" theories. All he asked was that God be left at the beginning. He granted that Darwin, mainly for the sake of decorum, gave his Victorian readers the option of a Deity who initially "breathed" life into a few forms. Darwin, strictly speaking, does not deny God. But, in Pusey's estimation, he does something worse: He makes God irrelevant. And this has been a serious consequence of Darwin's theory: the elimination of God as far as possible from our thoughts about creation. The victims of this intellectual blackout include everyone from the man on the street to serious Christian theologians.

In recent decades, Cardinal Joseph Ratzinger has been an eloquent and urgent advocate for the restoration of the doctrine of creation. Man is a creature — a contingent being inhabiting a universe that is itself highly contingent. This is the most important fact about him. Yet, the doctrine of creation has virtually disappeared from catechesis, preaching, and even theology. Ratzinger argues that until Catholics regain a sense of theological wonder at the fact of creation they will remain susceptible to the toxic cultural viruses floating around our radically secular culture.

A New Theology of Creation

A new theology of creation will not be a simple task. It will have to deal adroitly with the intellectual confidence games played by scientism. It will have to reintroduce modern science to Catholic metaphysics while avoiding anything smacking of a "Christian science." And it will have to deal with an unspoken tendency even among Catholics to cling to something less than a full idea of creation. Creation implies the sovereignty of a Creator, and modern man does not like authority. He prefers to make his own rules. The proposal to Adam and Eve in the Garden will always have resonance: Man, rather than God, gets to decide what is right and wrong. But this attempt at a radical human autonomy is bad metaphysics: It ignores the fact that in God "we live and move and have our being." It is also a formula for unhappiness. God is only interested in our own good, both now and in eternity, and this good can be anchored only in objective truths that we ourselves do not create.

This new theology of creation, then, may be "personalist" as well as cosmological. It will take its cue from the *Cat-*

echism of the Catholic Church, which has the personalist approach of John Paul II stamped all over it. The last universal catechism, issued after the Council of Trent, took the top-down, cosmological approach: God created the universe; it's his universe; these are his rules. A perfectly valid approach, except that it's not going to resonate with people who think that moral values, like ice-cream flavors, are a matter of private choice.

The new *Catechism* is personalist rather than cosmological. Near the beginning there is a quote from St. Augustine. As a young man, St. Augustine was tortured by the question "What will make me happy?" In attempting to answer it, he tried everything from recreational sex to the fourth-century equivalent of the New Age movement. None of it worked, of course, and in his *Confessions* he makes the famous admission that stands as an epigraph for all personalist thinking: "We were made for thee, O Lord, and our hearts are restless until they rest in thee."

Like St. Augustine, John Paul knows that the big questions about man cannot be answered apart from the God-question. But he is also aware that he is addressing a post-Christian society, one easily made nervous by the G-word. So, instead of starting with God, the pope's Christian personalism starts with man. It moves through a hierarchy of intermediate truths touching on man's happiness, leading gently but inexorably to his ultimate good, which is God.

This approach makes the Church's moral teachings far more accessible to our contemporaries. John Paul has a way of presenting unchanging truths that is light-years from the alienating legalisms that handicapped Catholic teaching a generation ago. And he starts with a simple proposition: Behind every "No" in the moral commandments there is an even greater "Yes." This, it seems to me, is the direction for a new theology of creation to take: Creation is a gift, and it is for our own good that we respond to this gift. To be created is to "enter into being," which means entering into a relation with the author of being. The more deeply our lives acknowledge this relationship, the better off we are.

The Christian Birth of Science

As a strictly philosophical proposition, creation has always been an unsettling idea. This is one reason why materialistic philosophies that dispense with it are so appealing. The notion that the universe had a beginning with time is one of the most radical concepts introduced by Christianity into the mind of the West. The Fourth Lateran Council defined it as dogma in 1215. It is an idea that would have scandalized an ancient Greek, who thought matter eternal, as much as a nineteenth-century positivist. Today, the notion that the universe had a beginning with, and not in, time is a commonplace of astrophysics. But science will never be able to pin down the "first" moment. It will approach it asymptotically, but never grasp it. (A trick question I ask my catechism class: What was God doing before he created the universe? Answer: Nothing; there was no "before" because there was no time.)

Paradoxically, although modern scientific dogmas like Darwinism are antagonistic to the idea of creation, it was the Catholic doctrine of creation that made modern science possible in the first place. Catholics ought to be aware of this simple historical fact, which is seldom mentioned in textbooks: Without Christianity there would be no science. As Stanley Jaki has brilliantly demonstrated in books like *The Savior of Science*, science was "stillborn" in every culture — Greek, Hindu, Chinese — except the Christian West. Science is a precarious enterprise that cannot get off the ground unless first given permission by philosophers and theologians. And this permission has been granted but once in history: by the great Catholic thinkers of the Middle Ages.

What is it about Christianity, and medieval Scholasticism in particular, that paved the way for Newton and Einstein?

First, the belief that the universe is rational. It was created through the Word, the divine Logos, which is rationality itself. When we read pagan accounts of the origin of the world, we find nothing but chaos. In the ancient Babylonian account, the universe, instead of being the deliberate act of an all-wise Creator, is the accidental by-product of a drunken orgy. The Greek gods are more decorous, but even they decide things mainly by quarrels and deception — not by a single, definitive *fiat*.

Second, the Catholic philosophers of the Middle Ages formulated a realist metaphysics, without which science is impossible. Catholics believe in the reality of matter. The physical world is not a veil of illusion, as the Eastern religions would have it, but an order of being that has its own dignity and built-in laws. Buddhist science for this reason is a nonstarter.

Third, Christians believe that history is linear and not (again as Eastern religions hold) cyclical. Only a universe with a beginning, middle, and end is hospitable to irreversible processes like the second law of thermodynamics. The work of Newton and Einstein would have been impossible without this simple assumption.

The Birth of Modern Cosmology

When Einstein formulated the general theory of relativity, which deals with gravity and the curvature of space, he was perturbed that his equations showed an expanding universe, which points to (but does not prove) a beginning. So he introduced a fudge factor, the "cosmological constant," to keep the cosmos static. He later called this "the biggest mistake of my life." When Edwin Hubble, the American astronomer, published data in 1931 showing that the universe was indeed expanding, Einstein finally accepted "the need for a beginning." When in 1964 two Bell Lab scientists in New Jersey accidentally discovered the three-degree background radiation, which can only be explained as the remnant of a superheated Big Bang, modern cosmology came of age — and found Catholic theology waiting there all along.

The universe began (we think) with an "initial singularity": All matter was packed into an infinitely dense point. The Big Bang, which may have occurred twelve billion years ago, must not be pictured as the expansion of matter within already existing space; rather, space, time, and matter came into existence simultaneously, a fact that would not have surprised St. Augustine. What Jaki calls the "specificity" of the formation of the universe is breathtaking. If the cosmic expansion had been a fraction less intense, it would have imploded billions of years ago; a fraction more intense, and the galaxies would not have formed. Picture a wall with thousands of dials; each must be at exactly the right setting — within a tolerance of millionths — in order for carbon-based life to eventually emerge in a suburb of the Milky Way. You cannot help but think of a Creator.

Einstein's universe, which is finite and highly specific, presents an enormous opportunity for the rearticulation of the cosmological argument for the existence of God. Although the universe points strongly to its contingency on a Creator, Catholics — it cannot be emphasized enough — have to be careful not to fall into the trap of "creation science" about which St. Augustine warned. Creation is a strictly philosophical concept; it has nothing to do with science, which deals only with quantitative matter. God's act of creation can in no way be caught by science's recording instruments.

Catholics also have to avoid the trap of biblical concordism, which is the attempt to fit the findings of modern science into the creation narrative of Genesis 1. Since the time of the Church Fathers, every theologian who has attempted this has found his clever scheme of concordance made obsolete by later science. Our own modern cosmology, which has trouble explaining many phenomena, such as the apparent distribution of matter in the universe, may someday be retired. So there is no need to think that when God said, "Let there be light!" he was referring to the burst of gamma rays that presumably occurred after the Big Bang. There were no gamma rays in ancient Hebrew cosmology.

The Act of Creation

Besides, we depart from scientific cosmology altogether when we consider the divine act of creation that brought the cosmos into being. We also dispense with the Divine Watchmaker of Anglican theology. The image of Watchmaker does not begin to address the mystery of the act of creation. Creation is an act unlike any human act. Human acts, such as watchmaking, involve movement from point A to point B — a change in an already existing state of being. But divine creation is the production of being itself — an act without movement, something that we cannot begin to imagine. God, who is pure act-of-being, causes finite acts-of-being. And he alone can do it. This is a far greater metaphysical truth than any "design" to be found in nature. In stalking Paley's Watchmaker, Darwin was pursuing the truncated divinity of Anglican theology and not the God who told Moses that he was being itself.

The Creator who revealed himself to Moses as pure being — "I am who am" (Exodus 3:14) — infinitely transcends his attributes as Watchmaker. He cannot be reduced to a mechanic who wound up the universe and then retired from the scene. And his creation cannot be thought of as simply inert matter set in motion. Creation, rather, partakes at each moment in the dynamism of the divine act-of-being. The visible world is shot through with it. When St. Augustine said that God is closer to us than we are to ourselves, he was speaking metaphysics, not poetry. Like all creation, including the angels, we tend unceasingly toward nothingness from which we are preserved at each instant by our Creator. We cannot keep ourselves in existence. Nor do we possess any perfection or goodness that we do not receive.

The fact that God is in all things, however, does not mean that all things are God. Even though we derive our act-of-being from God, we possess it in a participated and finite way that keeps us at an infinite distance from our Creator. At the same time, although we are radically contingent on God, who is intimately present in our being, we nonetheless are free. God wills to us our own freedom and respects the use we make of it. He both governs us and leaves us free. On the issue of free will, neither Calvin nor modern behaviorists are correct. As Dr. Johnson said to Boswell: "Why, sir, we *know* our will is free, and there's an end on't."

Darwin, who, by his own admission, got easily lost in the thickets of metaphysics, never treated seriously the doctrine of creation, which, in any event, had been watered down by Anglican theology. But what his theory did was to desensitize modern man to the deeper ontological realities. His book created an intellectual atmosphere where it is taken for granted that the word "evolution" banishes any discussion of creation. It does no such thing, of course. Even if Darwin's materialistic explanation of the origin of species were true, it would not move us any closer to answering the question "Why is there something rather than nothing?" Atheist scientists like Richard Dawkins who imply otherwise either are being dishonest or are suffering a serious philosophical blindness.

The Death of Darwinism

Darwin's explanation of the origin of species will nonetheless someday be retired. Whether this will happen rapidly (in the form of a Kuhnian paradigm shift) or gradually, one cannot say. A striking feature of the history of the theory is the persistence over almost a century and a half of an informed opposition among scientists. This never happens in the case of valid scientific theories, which are universally accepted within a generation or two of their formulation. Such opposition to Darwin exists today and seems to be growing.

The Catholic side of the debate over evolution should be calm and charitable. There is a revealing asymmetry in discussions between a well-informed Catholic and a scientific materialist. The latter often becomes heated and belligerent. This lack of serenity is increasingly noticeable in the Darwinist camp, and is a tip-off of the serious flaws in their position.

As Catholics, we should look forward to advances in science with enjoyment and confidence. And as nonscientific laymen, we should not hesitate to get involved in the debate over evolution, every aspect of which is accessible to the layman. A Catholic with some knowledge of his Thomistic heritage is more equipped than most to deal with the issue, which is philosophical as well as scientific. Nor should we leave popular science writing to people like Carl Sagan, Stephen Jay Gould, or Richard Dawkins, whose charming expositions, in

Stanley Jaki's phrase, "mask a fierce counter-metaphysics." These writers are masters of what Darwin called the "slow and silent side attacks" against Christianity. But they are fighting a rearguard action against the dissolution of the nineteenth-century materialist worldview.

Suggested Reading

The literature on Darwin is voluminous and growing. The following are suggestions for further reading under each chapter heading. The references are to the general bibliography.

Chapter One: Darwin and His Theory
The best general biography of Darwin is Desmond and Moore (1991), while the best intellectual biography remains the masterful study of Gertrude Himmelfarb (1959). A lighter read about Darwin and other early evolutionists is Eiseley (1958). Two good detailed accounts of the history of Darwin's theory are Depew and Weber (1995) and Lovtrup (1987). Lovtrup is a Swedish biologist whose close examination of the writings of Darwin and his disciples are devastating. Peter Bowler's several volumes are also well researched and informative.

Chapter Two: What the Fossils Show
The best general introduction to the paleontological evidence is Stanley (1981). Eldredge (1995) and Raup (1991) are also readable. Bird's encyclopedic volume (1989) is chock-full of quotations from evolutionists about the problems with the fossil record in their special areas. Schindewolf (1993) and Grasse (1977) are more demanding; however, their unbiased reading of the fossil record carries weight; both men were world-renowned scientists and neither could remotely be described as a creationist.

Chapter Three: Other Problems with Darwin's Theory
The best general critiques of Darwin's theory are Barzun (1958), Macbeth (1971), Denton (1986), Johnson (1991), and

Behe (1996). The chapter on Darwin in Belloc (1926) has lost none of its edge. Lunn (1951) contains some very well written chapters on Darwinism along with a good general critique of scientism. ReMine (1993), while employing some dubious metaphysical arguments, is voluminous and amply documented, as is Bird (1989). The problem of the numerical improbabilities of Darwin's theory are discussed in Moorhead and Kaplan (1967), which includes the proceedings of a scientific conference where a number of evolutionists and mathematicians voiced dissatisfaction with neo-Darwinism. Augros and Stanciu (1987) covers many of the problems of Darwinism and is very readable.

Chapter Four: Darwin's "One Long Argument"

Macbeth (1971) contains a clear and astringent discussion of the logical fallacies of the theory of natural selection. Brady (1982) is a more scholarly treatment of the problem. Grene (1974) treats the issue from a philosophical perspective. Lovtrup (1987) exposes the gaps of logic in the *Origin* with wit and acuity.

Chapter Five: Darwinism Since Darwin

See Chapter One above for histories of Darwinism. Hull (1973) is a valuable collection of essays by Darwin's early critics and supporters. For the vagaries of neo-Darwinism, see Grene (1974, 1983), Gould (1980), and Eldredge (1985). The attacks by Gould (1997) on what he calls Darwinian fundamentalism should alert even the mildly curious that all is not well with Darwinian orthodoxy. The classic works of neo-Darwinism are still worth reading, especially Simpson (1944). Eldredge (1985) is the most comprehensive presentation of the theory of punctuated equilibrium; its appendix contains the original 1972 essay, "Punctuated Equilibria: An Alternative to Phyletic Gradualism," in which Eldredge and Gould proposed the theory, which I submit is really a refutation of Darwinism, rather than a patch.

Chapter Six: The Question of Human Origins

Lewin (1997) is the best general book on the subject of prehuman fossils. The article by Cartmill, Pilbeam, and Isaac (1986) is a brief overview. Eldredge and Tattersall (1982) and Tattersall (1995) are iconoclastic, in that they challenge the standard picture of a smooth cascade of fossils leading from apes and humans; but they assume materialistic evolution did the job somehow. Stove (1995) has some devastating things to say about Darwinian explanations of human behavior. He is also very funny. Lubenow (1992) gives a creationist reading of the hominid fossil record. The chapter in Johnson (1991) on human paleontology is also good.

Chapter Seven: Darwinism as a Modern Ideology

Chesterton's many writings on Darwinism contain some of the best treatment of Darwinism as an ideology. See also Grene (1974) and Stove (1995). On Darwinism as a crypto-religion, see Lunn (1951) and Macbeth (1971). Stanley Jaki is also good on the subject, although his comments are scattered through his many volumes.

Chapter Eight: The Catholic Church and Evolution

Mivart (1871) and Behe (1996) are two good critiques of Darwinism written by Catholic biologists. The entry in the *Catholic Encyclopedia* (1907) is far more astute than its successor in the *New Catholic Encyclopedia* (1967). Jaki (1992) is a brilliant history of how theologians throughout history have handled, and mishandled, Genesis 1. Jaki's reading of Genesis 1 in light of ancient Hebrew cosmology is convincing. The easiest way to get papal documents is via the Internet or through the Daughters of St. Paul Bookstores.

Chapter Nine: Modern Christian Writers and Darwin

The relevant works of the authors treated in this chapter are in the bibliography. The striking point about these very disparate thinkers is that they agree that the theory of biological evolution does not contradict the Christian doctrine of creation. Of course, they all have a problem with evolutionary materialism. If I had to pick one book from this group of writers, it would be Chesterton (1925). The great merit of Gilson (1984) is that it makes clear that the real debate is not over evolution, but teleology. Numbers (1992) has an account of C. S. Lewis's dealings with British antievolutionists.

Chapter Ten: The Mystery of Creation

Ratzinger (1990) is a short but profound plea for the restoration of the doctrine of creation. He touches lightly on some of the issues raised by the scientific theory of evolution, but is mainly interested in the philosophical aspects of the problem. Gilson (1956) has an extensive chapter on St. Thomas's discussion of creation.

Bibliography

Ambrose, E. J., 1990, *The Mirror of Creation*, Scottish Academic Press, Edinburgh.

Augros, R. and Stanciu, G., 1987, *The New Biology*, Shambhala Publications, Boston.

Augustine, St., 1982, *The Literal Meaning of Genesis*, translated by John Hammond Taylor, in *Ancient Christian Writers* nos. 41 and 42, Newman Press, New York.

Barzun, Jacques, 1958, *Darwin, Marx, Wagner*, revised second edition, Doubleday Anchor, Garden City, N.Y.

Baum, R. F., 1988, *Doctors of Modernity: Darwin, Marx & Freud*, Sherwood Sugden, Peru, Ill.

Behe, Michael J., 1996, *Darwin's Black Box: The Biochemical Challenge to Evolution*, Free Press, New York.

Belloc, Hilaire, 1926, *A Companion to H. G. Wells's 'Outline of History,'* Sheed and Ward, London.

_____, 1926, *Mr. Belloc Still Objects*, Sheed and Ward, London.

Bertalanffy, Ludwig von, 1952, *Problems of Life*, Watts and Co., London.

_____, 1975, *Perspectives on General System Theory*, George Braziller, New York.

Bethell, Tom, 1985, "Agnostic Evolutionists," reprinted in Bethell, 1988, *The Electric Windmill*, Regnery, Washington, D. C.

Bird, W. R., 1989, *The Origin of Species Revisited*, two volumes, Philosophical Library, New York.

Bowler, Peter J., 1983, *The Eclipse of Darwinism*, Johns Hopkins University Press, Baltimore, Md.

_____, 1989, *Evolution: The History of an Idea*, revised edition, University of California Press, Berkeley.

_____, 1990, *Charles Darwin: The Man and His Influence*, Cambridge University Press, New York.

Brady, Ronald H., 1979, "Natural Selection and the Criteria by which a Theory is Judged," Systematic Zoology, 28:600-620.

_____, 1982, "Dogma and Doubt," *Biological Journal of the Linnean Society*, 17:79-86.

Buell, J. and Hearn, V., 1994, *Darwinism: Science or Philosophy?*, Foundation for Thought and Ethics, Richardson, Texas.

Butler, Samuel, 1879, *Evolution Old and New*, Hardwicke and Brogue, London.

_____, 1886, *Luck or Cunning*, Fifield, London.

_____, 1983, *Essays on Life, Art and Science* (original edition, 1908), Chelsea House, New York.

Campbell, Bernard, 1988, *Human Evolution: An Introduction to Man's Adaptations*, Aldine, New York.

Cartmill, M., Pilbeam, D., and Isaac, G., 1986, "One Hundred Years of Paleontology," *American Scientist*, 74:410-420.

Cassirer, Ernst, 1950, *The Problem of Knowledge*, Yale University Press, New Haven, Conn.

Catholic Encyclopedia, 1907, Robert Appleton, New York.

Chesterton, G. K., 1909, *Orthodoxy*, John Lane, London.

_____, 1910, *What's Wrong with the World*, Dodd, Mead, New York.

_____, 1923, *Fancies versus Fads*, Dodd, Mead, New York.

_____, 1925, *The Everlasting Man*, Doubleday, Garden City, N.Y.

_____, 1931, *Come to Think of It*, Dodd, Mead, New York.

Coren, Michael, 1993, *The Invisible Man: The Life and Liberties of H.G. Wells*, Atheneum, New York.

Darlington, C. D., 1961, *Darwin's Place in History*, Macmillan, New York.

Darwin, Charles, 1859, *The Origin of Species*, facsimile of the first edition, 1964, Harvard University Press, Cambridge, Mass.

_____, 1868, *The Variation of Animals and Plants under Domestication*, Murray, London.

_____, 1974, *Darwin's Early and Unpublished Notebooks*, transcribed and annotated by P. H. Barrett, Dutton, New York.

Davis, P. and Kenyon, D., 1989, *Of Pandas and People*, Haughton Publishing, Dallas, Tex.

Dawkins, Richard, 1976, *The Selfish Gene*, Oxford University Press, Inc., New York.

_____, 1986, *The Blind Watchmaker: Why the Evidence of Evolution Reveals a Universe without Design*, W. W. Norton Company, New York.

de Beer, G. R., 1963, *Charles Darwin: Evolution by Natural Selection*, Thomas Nelson, London.

Dennett, Daniel C., 1995, *Darwin's Dangerous Idea*, Simon and Schuster, New York.

Denton, Michael, 1986, *Evolution: A Theory in Crisis*, Adler and Adler, Bethesda, Md.

Depew, D. J. and Weber, B. H., eds., 1985, *Evolution at a Crossroads: The New Biology and the New Philosophy of Science*, MIT Press, Cambridge, Mass.

Depew, D. J. and Weber, B. H., 1995, *Darwinism Evolving*, MIT Press, Cambridge, Mass.

Desmond, A. and Moore, J., 1991, *Darwin: The Life of a Tormented Evolutionist*, Warner Books, New York.

Dewar, Douglas, 1931, *Difficulties of the Evolution Theory*, Edward Arnold, London.

Dewey, John, 1910, *The Influence of Darwin on Philosophy and Other Essays in Contemporary Thought*, Henry Holt, New York.

Dobzhansky, Theodosius, 1962, *Mankind Evolving: The Evo-*

lution of the Human Species, Yale University Press, New Haven, Conn.

_____, 1970, *Genetics of the Evolutionary Process*, Columbia University Press, New York.

_____, 1975, book review in *Evolution*, 29:376-378.

Driesch, Hans, 1908, *The Science and Philosophy of the Organism*, Black, London.

Eiseley, Loren, 1958, *Darwin's Century: Evolution and the Men Who Discovered It*, Doubleday, Garden City, N.Y.

Eldredge, Niles, 1982, *The Monkey Business: A Scientist Looks at Creationism*, Washington Square Press, New York.

_____, 1985, *Time Frames: The Rethinking of Darwinian Evolution and the Theory of Punctuated Equilibria*, Simon and Schuster, New York.

_____, 1985, *Unfinished Synthesis: Biological Hierarchies and Modern Evolutionary Thought*, Oxford University Press, Inc., New York.

_____, 1989, *Macro-Evolutionary Dynamics: Species, Niches, and Adaptive Peaks*, McGraw-Hill, New York.

_____, 1995, *Reinventing Darwin: The Great Debate at the High Table of Evolutionary Theory*, John Wiley and Sons, New York.

_____ and Cracraft, J., 1980, *Phylogenetic Patterns and the Evolutionary Process: Method and Theory in Comparative Biology*, Columbia University Press, New York.

_____ and Gould, S. J., 1972, "Punctuated Equilibria: An Alternative to Phyletic Gradualism," reprinted in Eldredge (1985).

_____ and Tattersall, I., 1982, *The Myths of Human Evolution*, Columbia University Press, New York.

Fisher, R. A., 1930, *The Genetical Theory of Natural Selection*, Clarendon Press, Oxford University Press, Inc., New York.

Gilson, Étienne, 1956, *The Christian Philosophy of St. Thomas Aquinas*, Random House, New York.

_____, 1984, *From Aristotle to Darwin and Back Again: A Journey in Final Causality, Species, and Evolution* (originally published as *D'Aristote à Darwin et retour*, Librairie Philosophique J. Vrin, Paris, 1971), University of Notre Dame Press, Notre Dame, Ind.

Glick, Thomas, ed., 1988, *The Comparative Reception of Darwinism*, with a new preface, University of Chicago Press, Chicago.

Goldschmidt, Richard, 1940, *The Material Basis of Evolution*, reissued in 1982 with an introduction by Stephen Jay Gould, Yale University Press, New Haven, Conn.

Gould, Stephen Jay, 1973, *Ever Since Darwin*, W. W. Norton, New York.

_____, 1980, *The Panda's Thumb*, W. W. Norton, New York.

_____, 1980, "Is a new and general theory of evolution emerging?" *Paleobiology* 6:119-130.

_____, 1980, "G. G. Simpson, paleontology, and the modern synthesis," in E. Mayr and W. B. Provine (1982).

_____, 1982, "Darwinism and the Expansion of Evolutionary Theory," *Science*, vol. 216, April 23, pp. 380-387.

_____, 1983, "The Hardening of the Synthesis," in Grene (1983), pp. 153-171.

_____, 1986, "Evolution and the Triumph of Homology, or Why History Matters," *American Scientist*, January-February, 74:60-69.

_____, 1991, *Bully for Brontosaurus*, W. W. Norton, New York.

_____, 1993, *Eight Little Piggies*, W. W. Norton, New York.

_____, 1995, *Dinosaur in a Haystack*, Harmony Books, Crown Publishers, New York.

_____, 1997, "The Darwinian Fundamentalists," *New York Review of Books*, vol. xliv, no. 10, June 12, 34-37.

_____, 1997, "The Pleasures of Pluralism," *New York Review of Books*, vol. xliv, no. 11, June 26, 47-52.

_____ and Eldredge, N., 1977, "Punctuated Equilibria: the tempo and mode of evolution reconsidered," *Paleobiology* 3:115, 147.

_____ and Lewontin, R. C., 1984, "The Spandrels of San Marco and the Panglossian Paradigm: A Critique of the Adaptionist Programme," *Proceedings of the Royal Society* (London) 205:581-598.

Grasse, Pierre P., 1977, *The Evolution of Living Organisms*, Academic Press, New York.

Grene, Marjorie, 1974, *The Understanding of Nature: Essays in the Philosophy of Biology*, D. Reidel Publishing, Boston.

_____, ed., 1983, *Dimensions of Darwinism: Themes and Counterthemes in Twentieth Century Evolutionary Theory*, Cambridge University Press, New York.

_____, 1987, "Hierarchies in Biology," *American Scientist*, 75:504-510.

Himmelfarb, Gertrude, 1959, *Darwin and the Darwinian Revolution*, W. W. Norton, New York.

Ho, M. and Sanders, P. T., eds., 1984, *Beyond Neo-Darwinism: An Introduction to the New Evolutionary Paradigm*, Academic Press, New York.

Hofstadter, Richard, 1955, *Social Darwinism in American Thought*, Beacon Press, Boston.

Hull, David L. ed., 1973, *Darwin and Critics: The Reception of Darwin's Theory of Evolution by the Scientific Community*, Harvard University Press, Cambridge, Mass.

_____, 1989, *The Metaphysics of Evolution*, State University of New York Press, Albany, N.Y.

Huxley, Aldous, 1937, *Ends and Means*, Chatto and Windus, London.

Huxley, J. S., 1942, *Evolution: The Modern Synthesis*, Allen and Unwin, London.

Huxley, T. H., 1863, *Man's Place in Nature*, London, reprinted in Huxley, *Collected Essays*, vol. 7.

_____, 1893-1894, *Collected Essays*, Macmillan, London.

Jaki, Stanley, 1978, *The Road of Science and the Ways to God*, University of Chicago Press, Chicago.

_____, 1983, *Apes, Angels, & Men*, Sherwood Sugden, La Salle, Ill.

_____, 1986, *Chance or Reality and Other Essays*, University of America Press, Lanham, Md.

_____, 1986, *Chesterton: A Seer of Science*, University of Illinois Press, Urbana, Ill.

_____, 1988, *The Absolute Beneath the Relative and Other Essays*, University of America Press, Lanham, Md.

_____, 1988, *The Savior of Science*, Regnery, Washington, D.C.

_____, 1990, *The Purpose of It All*, Regnery, Washington, D.C.

_____, 1991, "Newman and Evolution," *Downside Review*, Exeter, England, January.

_____, 1992, *Genesis 1 Through the Ages*, Thomas More Press, London.

_____, 1996, *Bible and Science*, Christendom Press, Front Royal, Va.

Johnson, Phillip, 1991, *Darwin on Trial*, Regnery, Washington, D.C.

Kaufmann, Walter, 1968, *Nietzsche: Philosopher, Psychologist, Antichrist* (fourth edition), Princeton University Press, Princeton, N.J.

Kuhn, Thomas, 1970, *The Structure of Scientific Revolutions*, second edition, enlarged, University of Chicago Press, Chicago.

Langford, Jerome J., 1971, *Galileo, Science and the Church*, third edition, University of Michigan Press, Ann Arbor, Mich.

Lewin, Roger, 1997, *Bones of Contention*, second edition, University of Chicago Press, Chicago.

Lewis, C. S., 1947, *Miracles*, Macmillan, New York.

_____, 1967, "The Funeral of a Great Myth," published posthumously in *Christian Reflections*, William B. Eerdmans, Grand Rapids, Mich.

Lewontin, Richard, 1974, *The Genetic Basis of Evolutionary Change*, Columbia University Press, New York.

Lovtrup, Soren, 1987, *Darwinism: The Refutation of a Myth*, Croom Helm, London.

Lubenow, Marvin, 1992, *Bones of Contention: A Creationist Assessment of Human Fossils*, Baker Books, Grand Rapids, Mich.

Lunn, Arnold, 1951, *The Revolt Against Reason*, Sheed and Ward, New York.

Macbeth, Norman, 1971, *Darwin Retried: An Appeal to Reason*, Gambit Press, Ipswich, Mass.

_____, 1985, "The Hypothesis of Divergent Ancestry," *Historia Natura*, 5:321-326.

Maritain, Jacques, 1940, *Wisdom and Science*, Lowe and Brydone, London.

_____, 1951, *Philosophy of Nature*, Philosophical Library, New York.

_____, 1968, *The Peasant of the Garonne* (original French edition, 1966), Holt, Reinhart and Winston, New York.

_____, 1997, *Untrammeled Approaches* (original French edition, 1973), University of Notre Dame Press, Notre Dame, Ind.

Maynard Smith, John, 1975, *The Theory of Evolution*, third edition, Penguin Books, Viking Penguin, New York.

_____, 1983, "Current Controversies in Evolutionary Biology," in Grene (1983).

_____, 1984, "Paleontology at the High Table," *Nature*, 309:401-402.

Mayr, Ernst, 1942, *Systematics and the Origin of Species*, Columbia University Press, New York.

_____, 1963, *Animal Species and Evolution*, Belknap, Harvard University Press, Cambridge, Mass.

_____, 1976, *Evolution and the Diversity of Life*, Belknap, Harvard University Press, Cambridge, Mass.

_____, 1982, *The Growth of Biological Thought: Diversity, Evolution and Inheritance*, Belknap Press, Harvard University Press, Cambridge, Mass.

_____, 1988, *Toward a New Philosophy of Biology: Observations of an Evolutionist*, Belknap Press, Harvard University Press, Cambridge, Mass.

_____, 1991, *One Long Argument: Charles Darwin and the Genesis of Modern Evolutionary Thought*, Harvard University Press, Cambridge, Mass.

_____ and Provine, W. B., eds., 1980, *The Evolutionary Synthesis*, Harvard University Press, Cambridge, Mass.

Mendel, Gregor Johann, 1965, *Experiments on Plant Hybridization*, Harvard University Press, Cambridge, Mass.

Mivart, St. George, 1871, *On the Genesis of Species*, Macmillan, London.

Monod, Jacques, 1971, *Chance and Necessity* (original French edition, 1979), Knopf, New York.

Moorhead, P. S. and Kaplan, M. M., eds., 1967, *Mathematical Challenges to the Neo-Darwinian Interpretation of Evolution*, Wistar Institute, Philadelphia.

More, Louis T., 1925, *The Dogma of Evolution*, Princeton University Press, Princeton, N.J.

Numbers, Ronald, 1992, *The Creationists: The Evolution of Scientific Creationism*, Knopf, New York.

Pilbeam, David, 1989, "Human Fossil History and Evolutionary Paradigms," in M. K. Hecht, ed., *Evolutionary Biology at the Crossroads*, Queens College Press, New York.

Popper, Karl, 1972, *Objective Knowledge*, Oxford University Press, Inc., New York.

_____, 1974, *Unended Quest: An Intellectual Autobiography*, in *The Philosophy of Karl Popper*, Open Court Publishing, La Salle, Ill.

_____, 1985, *Popper Selections*, edited by David Miller, Princeton University Press, Princeton, N.J.

Ratzinger, Joseph, 1990, *'In the Beginning . . .': A Catholic Understanding of the Story of Creation and the Fall*, Our Sunday Visitor, Inc., Huntington, Ind.

Raup, David, 1991, *Extinction: Bad Genes or Bad Luck?*, W. W. Norton, New York.

Reid, Robert G. B., 1985, *Evolutionary Theory: The Unfinished Synthesis*, Cornell University Press, Ithaca, N.Y.

ReMine, Walter James, 1993, *The Biotic Message: Evolution versus Message Theory*, St. Paul Science, St. Paul, Minn.

Santillana, G. de, 1955, *The Crime of Galileo*, University of Chicago, Chicago.

Schindewolf, Otto H., 1993, *Basic Questions in Paleontology* (original German edition, 1950), University of Chicago Press, Chicago.

Schmaus, Michael, 1969, *Dogma 2: God and Creation*, Sheed and Ward, London.

Shaw, George Bernard, 1919, *Heartbreak House*, Constable, London.

Sheed, F. J., 1978, *Theology and Sanity*, revised edition, Our Sunday Visitor, Inc., Huntington, Ind.

Simpson, G. G., 1944, *Tempo and Mode in Evolution*, Columbia University Press, New York.

_____, 1967, *The Meaning of Evolution*, revised edition, Yale University Press, New Haven, Conn.

Spengler, Oswald, 1939, *The Decline of the West*, 2 vols., reprinted by Knopf, New York.

Stanley, Steven, 1981, *The New Evolutionary Time Table: Fossils, Genes and the Origin of Species*, Basic Books, New York.

Stove, David, 1995, *Darwinian Fairytales*, Avebury, Aldershot, England.

Sulloway, Frank J., 1982, "Darwin and his Finches: The Evolution of a Legend," *Journal of the History of Biology*, vol. 15, no. 1, pp.1-53.

Swinton, W. E., 1960, *Biology and Comparative Physiology of Birds*, Academic Press, New York.

Tattersall, Ian, 1995, *The Fossil Trail*, Oxford University Press, Inc., New York.

Taylor, Gordon Rattray, 1983, *The Great Evolution Mystery*, Secker and Warburg, London.

Thompson, W. R., 1956, "Introduction," *Origin of Species*, Everyman Library No. 811, Sussex, England.

Vorzimmer, Peter J., 1970, *Charles Darwin: The Years of Controversy*, Temple University Press, Philadelphia.

Watson, E. L. Grant, 1964, *The Mystery of Life*, Abelard Schuman, London.

Weiner, Jonathan, 1994, *The Beak of the Finch*, Knopf, New York.

Wesson, Robert, 1991, *Beyond Natural Selection*, MIT Press, Cambridge, Mass.

Whitehead, A. N., 1925, *Science and the Modern World*, Macmillan, New York.

_____, 1937, *Adventures in Ideas*, Macmillan, New York.

Willey, Basil, 1960, *Darwin and Butler: Two Versions of Evolution*, Chatto and Windus, London.

Willis, J. C., 1940, *The Course of Evolution*, Cambridge University Press, London.

Wilson, A. N., 1984, *Hilaire Belloc: A Biography*, Atheneum, New York.

_____, 1990, *C. S. Lewis: A Biography*, Norton, New York.

Wilson, Edward O., 1978, *On Human Nature*, Harvard University Press, Cambridge, Mass.

_____, 1980, *Sociobiology*, abridged edition, Harvard University Press, Cambridge, Mass.

Zuckerman, Lord, 1991, "Apes R Not Us," *New York Review of Books*, vol. XXXVIII, no. 10, May 30.

Index of Proper Names

Our Sunday Visitor...
Your Source for Discovering the Riches of the Catholic Faith

Our Sunday Visitor has an extensive line of materials for young children, teens, and adults. Our books, Bibles, booklets, CD-ROMs, audios, and videos are available in bookstores worldwide.

To receive a FREE full-line catalog or for more information, call **Our Sunday Visitor** at **1-800-348-2440**. Or write, **Our Sunday Visitor** / 200 Noll Plaza / Huntington, IN 46750.

Please send me: __ A catalog
Please send me materials on:
   __ Apologetics and catechetics   __ Reference works
   __ Prayer books   __ Heritage and the saints
   __ The family   __ The parish

Name_____

Address_____Apt._____

City_____State___Zip_____

Telephone ( )_____
                                              A73BBABP

Please send a friend: __ A catalog
Please send a friend materials on:
   __ Apologetics and catechetics   __ Reference works
   __ Prayer books   __ Heritage and the saints
   __ The family   __ The parish

Name_____

Address_____Apt._____

City_____State___Zip_____

Telephone ( )_____
                                              A73BBABP

Our Sunday Visitor
200 Noll Plaza
Huntington, IN 46750
1-800-348-2440
OSVSALES@AOL.COM

Your Source for Discovering the Riches of the Catholic Faith

As George Sim Johnston tells us:

> Some Catholics take Darwin's account
> at face value and dismiss the early chap-
> ters of Genesis as myth or allegory. Others
> simply dig in their heels and refuse to
> accept any scientific datum, including the
> dating of fossils, that does not fit a literal
> reading of Genesis. For these "creation-
> ists" — Catholic as well as Protestant — it
> is evolution, and not the Book of Genesis,
> that is the fairy tale.
>
> There can be no real conflict between
> faith and the legitimate findings of sci-
> ence. Truth is indivisible, and the works of
> God cannot contradict what he has chosen
> to reveal through Scripture and Tradition.
> The danger occurs when scientists trespass
> into theology or vice versa.
>
> Today, science and religion are like
> two armed camps gazing suspiciously at
> one another across a huge metaphysical
> divide. But the fact is, they have much to
> talk about.
>
> "Evolution" is the idea that all life-
> forms share common ancestors, and maybe
> even a single ancestor. This is a reasonable,
> if unproven, hypothesis. It is reasonable
> not because anyone has ever seen a species
> turn into a new one (one hasn't), but
> because all life-forms share certain